THIS BOOK BELONGS TO

_____

START DATE

_____

SHE READS TRUTH

EXECUTIVE

FOUNDER/CHIEF EXECUTIVE OFFICER
Raechel Myers

CO-FOUNDER/CHIEF CONTENT OFFICER
Amanda Bible Williams

CHIEF OPERATING OFFICER
Ryan Myers

EDITORIAL

EDITORIAL DIRECTOR
Jessica Lamb

MANAGING EDITOR
Beth Joseph, MDiv

DIGITAL MANAGING EDITOR
Oghosa Iyamu, MDiv

ASSOCIATE EDITORS
Lindsey Jacobi, MDiv
Tameshia Williams, ThM

EDITORIAL ASSISTANT
Hannah Little, MTS

CREATIVE

CREATIVE DIRECTOR
Amy Dennis

ART DIRECTORS
Kelsea Allen
Aimee Lindamood

DESIGNERS
Abbey Benson
Amanda Brush, MA
Annie Glover
Lauren Haag

JUNIOR DESIGNER
Jessie Gerakinis

MARKETING

MARKETING DIRECTOR
Kamron Kunce

SOCIAL MEDIA STRATEGIST
Taylor Krupp

OPERATIONS

OPERATIONS DIRECTOR
Allison Sutton

OFFICE MANAGER
Nicole Quirion

PROJECT ASSISTANT
Mary Beth Montgomery

SHIPPING

FULFILLMENT LEAD
Cait Baggerman

FULFILLMENT SPECIALISTS
Kajsa Matheny
Noe Sanchez

SUBSCRIPTION INQUIRIES
orders@shereadstruth.com

COMMUNITY SUPPORT

COMMUNITY SUPPORT MANAGER
Kara Hewett, MOL

COMMUNITY SUPPORT SPECIALISTS
Katy McKnight
Heather Vollono
Margot Williams

CONTRIBUTORS

RECIPES
Shaw family (72)
Sugar Drop Bakery (140)

@SHEREADSTRUTH

Download the
She Reads Truth app,
available for iOS
and Android

Subscribe to the
She Reads Truth podcast

SHEREADSTRUTH.COM

SHE READS TRUTH™

© 2022 by She Reads Truth, LLC

All rights reserved.

All photography used by permission.

ISBN 978-1-952670-67-1

1 2 3 4 5 6 7 8 9 10

All Scripture is taken from the Christian Standard Bible®. Copyright © 2020 by Holman Bible Publishers. Used by permission. Christian Standard Bible® and CSB® are federally registered trademarks of Holman Bible Publishers.

Research support provided by Logos Bible Software™. Learn more at logos.com.

This book was printed offset in Nashville, Tennessee, on 70# Lynx Opaque. Cover is 100# Cougar Opaque with a spot UV and soft touch lamination.

ADVENT 2022

JOY OF EVERY LONGING HEART

SHE READS TRUTH

THE ONE WE'RE LONGING FOR IS JESUS.

Raechel Myers
FOUNDER/CHIEF
EXECUTIVE OFFICER

As a Michigander in the '90s, our snowy season often stretched from October to April. I remember shivering through Easter morning photos in my hat and gloves, celebrating spring with snow drifts in the church parking lot.

But Christmastime was where all that accumulation really worked to our advantage. We enjoyed snowy Christmas Eve walks down the middle of unplowed streets, snow forts big enough to gather friends inside, and meeting up with classmates at the best sledding hill in town.

Then we moved to Tennessee. And in the sixteen winters we have lived here, we've yet to see a white Christmas. Every year, my longing for the beauty of big flakes of falling snow begins the moment the dessert plates are cleared after Thanksgiving dinner and lasts until we finally see the first snowfall of winter, usually when we're back in Michigan visiting family.

When our She Reads Truth team started dreaming about Advent 2022, we turned to the lyrics of the hymn "Come, Thou Long-Expected Jesus," (which happens to be both Amanda's and my all-time favorite Christmas carol). The line, "joy of ev'ry longing heart" connected with us deeply. We thought about all the longing hearts across the world and through time, and about every man, woman, and child who will read Scripture with us this Advent season. Every one of us, without exception, knows what it means to long for someone or something. But like snow at Christmastime, the earthly things we long for eventually fade away, or fail to satisfy, or possibly never come to fruition at all. That's because the deep-rooted longing of every human heart can only be satisfied by the God who created us. The One we're longing for is Jesus.

Advent is a season for preparing our hearts to celebrate the birth of Jesus Christ. Alongside the women and men of the Old Testament who looked forward to the promised Messiah, and those in the early Church who lived on alert for His promised return, we look to the only One who will never change, never fail us, never fade away.

I encourage you, in this season marked by longing for "things," to begin your Advent journey by examining exactly what it is you're longing for. Ask yourself what your heart truly desires. And as you journey with us through the lyrics of this old hymn and the ancient, timeless words of Scripture, ask the God who came to dwell with us to align your longings with His and satisfy your heart in Him.

This book was made with you in mind, and our team has prayed for you all along the way as we created it. May you anticipate and be satisfied by the God who came to us as a baby and will one day return in glory—Jesus, the joy of every longing heart.

DESIGN ON PURPOSE

At She Reads Truth, we believe in pairing the inherently beautiful Word of God with the aesthetic beauty it deserves. Each of our resources is thoughtfully and artfully designed to highlight the beauty, goodness, and truth of Scripture in a way that reflects the themes of each curated reading plan.

The Advent 2022 Study Book explores the coming of Christ—both His first and second advents—through the lens of a classic, nostalgic hymn.

This approach inspired us to incorporate a color palette that is festive, yet unique. The pink tones are influenced by the traditional red color of Christmas and the baby blue hue is a fresh and modern take on classic Christmas green. These unconventional tones breathe fresh air into the aesthetic of this beloved season.

The layout for this Study Book was created to be festive, merry, and bright. The joy we feel as each calendar day inches us closer to Christmas is mirrored by joyful, new designs found at the turn of every page.

HOW TO USE THIS BOOK

She Reads Truth is a community of women dedicated to reading the Word of God every day. In this Advent 2022 reading plan, we will explore how Scripture presents Jesus as God who came to dwell among us, and as the One whose return we are longing for.

READ & REFLECT

Your Advent 2022 Study Book focuses primarily on Scripture, with bonus resources to facilitate deeper engagement with God's Word.

SCRIPTURE READING

Designed to begin on November 27 (the first Sunday of Advent), this Study Book presents daily Scripture readings for the 2022 Advent season, along with readings for the last week of the year.

REFLECTION QUESTIONS

Each weekday features prompts and questions for personal reflection.

COMMUNITY & CONVERSATION

The She Reads Truth community will start Day 1 of Advent 2022 on **Sunday, November 27, 2022.** Join women from Montpelier to Mexico as they read along with you!

 SHE READS TRUTH APP

Devotionals corresponding to each daily reading can be found in the Advent 2022 reading plan on the She Reads Truth app. New devotionals will be published each weekday once the plan begins on **Sunday, November 27, 2022. You can use the app to participate in community discussion and more.**

GRACE DAY

Use Saturdays to catch up on your reading, pray, and rest in the presence of the Lord.

SUNDAYS

Each Sunday features a holiday hymn with a short reflection and a related passage of Scripture.

EXTRAS

This book features additional tools to help you gain a deeper understanding of the text.

Find a complete list of extras on page 13.

 **SHEREADSTRUTH.COM**

The Advent 2022 reading plan and devotionals will also be available at SheReadsTruth.com as the community reads each day. Invite your family, friends, and neighbors to read along with you!

 SHE READS TRUTH PODCAST

Subscribe to the She Reads Truth podcast and join our founders and their guests each week as they talk about the beauty, goodness, and truth they find in Scripture.

 *Podcast episodes 156–160 for our Advent 2022 series release on Mondays beginning **November 28, 2022**.*

TABLE
OF
CONTENTS

The **Advent 2022: Joy of Every Longing Heart** reading plan is inspired by the lyrics of "Come, Thou Long-Expected Jesus." Each day will explore thematic Scripture readings guided by the lyrics of the hymn, with some lyrics spanning multiple days.

week 04

week 05

"I AM THE ALPHA AND THE OMEGA," SAYS THE LORD GOD, "THE ONE WHO IS, WHO WAS, AND WHO IS TO COME, THE ALMIGHTY."

KEY VERSE

Revelation 1:8

WHAT IS ADVENT?

Advent is a Latin word that means "coming" or "arrival." Advent is a season of the Church calendar that stretches from four Sundays before Christmas Day through Christmas Eve.

It is a season full of hope, expectation, and longing.

This year, our Advent reading plan is guided by the lyrics of the hymn "Come, Thou Long-Expected Jesus." The words of this song situate us rightly as Christians—a people between two advents. We remember and celebrate the Son of God coming down to us, taking on humanity to be born as a baby in Bethlehem. And we anticipate His future, triumphant return as King of kings (Lk 2:11–15; Rv 21:5–7).

MARANATHA

(MAR-UH-NATH-UH)

Maranatha is an Aramaic word found in the New Testament (1Co 16:22) that is also sometimes used in connection to Advent. It means "the Lord has come!" or "Lord, come!" Arguments and evidence can be made for both translations, and yet the spirit of Advent holds both of these statements in tension. During the Advent season, we remember and declare that the hope of every longing heart has come in Jesus. Even still, we anticipate His second coming and the renewal of all things, crying, "Lord, come!"

God has always been the One to come to us. The key verse for this Advent study (Rv 1:8) reminds us that what is true of God's character and nature has always been and will always be true. Throughout this reading plan, we'll read New Testament passages that demonstrate how Jesus, the Son, is the embodiment of the God we experience throughout the Old Testament. The story of Christmas is a story of how the God of creation, the patriarchs, the prophets, and the marginalized took on human nature and came near to us. Where sin and shame created a barrier, He made a way for His people to be in His presence, conquering death and offering us reconciliation and salvation.

We also celebrate that God came to us again at Pentecost, when the Spirit—His very presence—came to dwell in and among God's people. His Spirit within us keeps us looking ahead, anticipating the second advent when Christ will return. So, during this Advent season, together we say, "maranatha!"

ADVENT
rhythms

During Advent, we intentionally practice slowing down our **rhythms**, taking time to contemplate Christ's first coming and long for His second.

Consider how to make intentional time and space to sit in God's presence during this season. Pray, asking God to meet with you in the midst of a holiday season that can be full of distraction and to-do lists. Reflect on the daily Scripture readings, inviting the words to instruct and ground you.

Use the space below to write out the rhythms you want to practice this Advent season.

RHYTHMS FOR THIS ADVENT SEASON

SLOWLY READ SCRIPTURE EACH DAY, MEDITATING ON GOD'S WORD

SPEND TIME DAILY IN PRAYER AND REFLECTION

EXTRA

Celebration is the practice of actively remembering and enjoying God in our lives. The spiritual discipline of celebration cultivates joy as we acknowledge the beauty, goodness, and truth that comes from God. During Advent, we also **celebrate** Christ's first coming and rejoice in the promise of His return.

Throughout this Study Book, you'll find opportunities to cultivate celebration. Whether through singing the Christmas hymns, making and sharing holiday recipes and crafts, or creating your own holiday activities and traditions, remember to make room for praise and thanksgiving.

Use the space below to write out the ways you want to celebrate this Advent season.

WAYS TO CELEBRATE THIS ADVENT SEASON

MAKE A DONATION—BIG OR SMALL—TO A PERSON, FAMILY, OR ORGANIZATION THAT MATTERS TO YOU

BAKE HOLIDAY COOKIES AND TREATS

celebrate

HOLIDAY calendar

2022

	SUNDAY	MONDAY	TUESDAY
NOVEMBER	**27** NOV ADVENT BEGINS	**28**	**29**
DECEMBER	**04** SECOND SUNDAY OF ADVENT	**05**	**06** DON'T FORGET! Today is the last day to order from ShopSheReadsTruth.com for standard shipping in time for Christmas!
DECEMBER	**11** THIRD SUNDAY OF ADVENT	**12**	**13**
DECEMBER	**18** FOURTH SUNDAY OF ADVENT	**19**	**20**
DECEMBER	**25** christmas DAY CHRISTMASTIDE BEGINS	**26**	**27**
JANUARY	**01** JAN SECOND SUNDAY OF CHRISTMASTIDE	**02** Start The Life of Jesus Study Book with the She Reads Truth community!	**03**

WEDNESDAY	THURSDAY	FRIDAY	SATURDAY
30 Browse your book for crafts and use this link to purchase supplies!	**01** DEC	**02**	**03** Don't forget to purchase any ingredients you need for your Advent recipes!
07	**08**	**09** *ADVENT PLAYLIST*	**10**
14	**15** *LAST DAY TO ORDER* The Life of Jesus Study Book for January!	**16**	**17**
21	**22**	**23**	**24** *christmas EVE*
28	**29** *FOR THE RECORD* Turn to page 182 to reflect on 2022 and pray for the year ahead.	**30**	**31**
04	**05**	**06** EPIPHANY	**07**

Day 1

THE FIRST SUNDAY
of Advent

When the time came to completion,
God sent his Son, born of a woman,
born under the law, to redeem those
under the law, so that we might
receive adoption as sons.

Galatians 4:4–5

Of the 6,000 hymns Charles Wesley wrote in his lifetime, "Come, Thou Long-Expected Jesus" is among his most beloved and well-known. Wesley composed the carol for his collection *Hymns for the Nativity of Our Lord*, its lyrics expressing many Advent themes and modeling the Israelites' waiting and longing for a King who would bring freedom, rest, strength, and consolation. The title of this Study Book comes from the lyric "joy of ev'ry longing heart."

Traditionally, this carol is sung on the first Sunday of Advent. We sing it today in joyful celebration of Christ's first coming, while at the same time longing and praying for His return.

COME, THOU LONG-EXPECTED JESUS

1. Come, Thou long-expected Jesus, Born to set Thy
2. Born Thy people to deliver, Born a child, and

people free; From our fears and sins release us;
yet a King, Born to reign in us forever,

Let us find our rest in Thee. Israel's strength and conso-
Now Thy gracious kingdom bring. By Thine own eternal

lation, Hope of all the earth Thou art; Dear desire of
Spirit rule in all our hearts alone; By Thine all-suf-

ev-'ry nation, Joy of ev-'ry longing heart.
ficient merit, Raise us to Thy glorious throne.

words
/ CHARLES WESLEY /

music
ROWLAND H. PRICHARD /

COME, THOU LONG-EXPECTED JESUS

DAY 2

GENESIS 3

THE TEMPTATION AND THE FALL

¹ Now the serpent was the most cunning of all the wild animals that the Lord God had made. He said to the woman, "Did God really say, 'You can't eat from any tree in the garden'?"

² The woman said to the serpent, "We may eat the fruit from the trees in the garden. ³ But about the fruit of the tree in the middle of the garden, God said, 'You must not eat it or touch it, or you will die.'"

⁴ "No! You will certainly not die," the serpent said to the woman. ⁵ "In fact, God knows that when you eat it your eyes will be opened and you will be like God, knowing good and evil." ⁶ The woman saw that the tree was good for food and delightful to look at, and that it was desirable for obtaining wisdom. So she took some of its fruit and ate it; she also gave some to her husband, who was with her, and he ate it. ⁷ Then the eyes of both of them were opened, and they knew they were naked; so they sewed fig leaves together and made coverings for themselves.

SIN'S CONSEQUENCES

⁸ Then the man and his wife heard the sound of the Lord God walking in the garden at the time of the evening breeze, and they hid from the Lord God among the trees of the garden. ⁹ So the Lord God called out to the man and said to him, "Where are you?"

¹⁰ And he said, "I heard you in the garden, and I was afraid because I was naked, so I hid."

¹¹ Then he asked, "Who told you that you were naked? Did you eat from the tree that I commanded you not to eat from?"

¹² The man replied, "The woman you gave to be with me—she gave me some fruit from the tree, and I ate."

¹³ So the Lord God asked the woman, "What have you done?"

And the woman said, "The serpent deceived me, and I ate."

¹⁴ So the Lord God said to the serpent:

Because you have done this,
you are cursed more than any livestock
and more than any wild animal.
You will move on your belly
and eat dust all the days of your life.
¹⁵ I will put hostility between you and the woman,
and between your offspring and her offspring.
He will strike your head,
and you will strike his heel.

¹⁶ He said to the woman:

I will intensify your labor pains;
you will bear children with painful effort.
Your desire will be for your husband,
yet he will rule over you.

[17] And he said to the man, "Because you listened to your wife and ate from the tree about which I commanded you, 'Do not eat from it':

The ground is cursed because of you.
You will eat from it by means of painful labor
all the days of your life.
[18] It will produce thorns and thistles for you,
and you will eat the plants of the field.
[19] You will eat bread by the sweat of your brow
until you return to the ground,
since you were taken from it.
For you are dust,
and you will return to dust."

[20] The man named his wife Eve because she was the mother of all the living. [21] The LORD God made clothing from skins for the man and his wife, and he clothed them.

[22] The LORD God said, "Since the man has become like one of us, knowing good and evil, he must not reach out, take from the tree of life, eat, and live forever." [23] So the LORD God sent him away from the garden of Eden to work the ground from which he was taken. [24] He drove the man out and stationed the cherubim and the flaming, whirling sword east of the garden of Eden to guard the way to the tree of life.

pause // Underline Genesis 3:8–9 and 21, God's pursuit of and care for Adam and Eve. Underline God's actions in 3:23–24. //

ROMANS 5:12-21

DEATH THROUGH ADAM AND LIFE THROUGH CHRIST

[12] Therefore, just as sin entered the world through one man, and death through sin, in this way death spread to all people, because all sinned. [13] In fact, sin was in the world before the law, but sin is not charged to a person's account when there is no law. [14] Nevertheless, death reigned from Adam to Moses, even over those who did not sin in the likeness of Adam's transgression. He is a type of the Coming One.

[15] But the gift is not like the trespass. For if by the one man's trespass the many died, how much more have the grace of God and the gift which comes through the grace of the one man Jesus Christ overflowed to the many. [16] And the gift is not like the one man's sin, because from one sin came the judgment, resulting in condemnation, but from many trespasses came the gift, resulting in justification. [17] If by the one man's trespass,

death reigned through that one man, how much more will those who receive the overflow of grace and the gift of righteousness reign in life through the one man, Jesus Christ.

[18] So then, as through one trespass there is condemnation for everyone, so also through one righteous act there is justification leading to life for everyone. [19] For just as through one man's disobedience the many were made sinners, so also through the one man's obedience the many will be made righteous. [20] The law came along to multiply the trespass. But where sin multiplied, grace multiplied even more [21] so that, just as sin reigned in death, so also grace will reign through righteousness, resulting in eternal life through Jesus Christ our Lord.

1 CORINTHIANS 15:45-49

[45] So it is written, The first man Adam became a living being; the last Adam became a life-giving spirit. [46] However, the spiritual is not first, but the natural, then the spiritual.

[47] The first man was from the earth, a man of dust; the second man is from heaven. [48] Like the man of dust, so are those who are of the dust; like the man of heaven, so are those who are of heaven. [49] And just as we have borne the image of the man of dust, we will also bear the image of the man of heaven.

COLOSSIANS 1:14-23

[14] In him we have redemption, the forgiveness of sins.

THE CENTRALITY OF CHRIST

[15] He is the image of the invisible God,
  the firstborn over all creation.

[16] For everything was created by him,
in heaven and on earth,
the visible and the invisible,
whether thrones or dominions
or rulers or authorities—
all things have been created through him and for him.
[17] He is before all things,
and by him all things hold together.
[18] He is also the head of the body, the church;
he is the beginning,
the firstborn from the dead,
so that he might come to have
first place in everything.
[19] For God was pleased to have
all his fullness dwell in him,
[20] and through him to reconcile
everything to himself,
whether things on earth or things in heaven,
by making peace
through his blood, shed on the cross.

[21] Once you were alienated and hostile in your minds as expressed in your evil actions. [22] But now he has reconciled you by his physical body through his death, to present you holy, faultless, and blameless before him— [23] if indeed you remain grounded and steadfast in the faith and are not shifted away from the hope of the gospel that you heard. This gospel has been proclaimed in all creation under heaven, and I, Paul, have become a servant of it.

REVELATION 1:8

"I am the Alpha and the Omega,"
says the Lord God, "the one who is,
who was, and who is to come,
the Almighty."

WHERE IN TODAY'S NEW TESTAMENT READING DO YOU SEE GOD'S PURSUIT? HOW DOES THE ADVENT SEASON CENTER US ON HIS CARE FOR US THROUGH CHRIST?

———————

Use the space below to respond,
reflect on the reading, journal, or record a prayer.

SONGS IN SCRIPTURE

Advent has long been associated with singing. We sing songs of reflection and celebration about Jesus's first coming and songs that look forward to His return. In the Gospels, the story of Jesus's birth includes multiple songs: from Mary, Zechariah, and Simeon. Songs also show up in other places in Scripture, and certain books like Psalms, Song of Songs, and Lamentations are composed entirely of poetry which can be sung.

Songs in the Bible cover the full range of emotions and call attention to the significance of an event or a particular truth. Here are some of the key songs found in Scripture.

Israel's Song

EX 15:1-18

The song Moses and the Israelites sang after crossing the Red Sea on dry land. This song recounts the story of Israel's miraculous escape from Egypt and the destruction of Pharaoh's army in the Red Sea.

Miriam's Song

EX 15:21

Miriam's response to Israel's song, calling the people to sing to the Lord who conquered their enemies.

The Song of the Well in the Desert

NM 21:17-18

The song Israel sang when they came to a well in the desert that the Lord had told Moses about.

The Song of Moses

DT 31:19-32:43

The song of blessing and warning Moses sings at the end of his life, summarizing the exodus and God's faithfulness to His people.

Deborah's Song

JDG 5

A song of victory sung by Deborah, the prophetess, and Barak after the Lord delivered Israel from the Canaanites.

The Song of David's Victory

1SM 18:7

The song the women of Israel sang, celebrating and elevating David's victories over King Saul's, which kindled Saul's jealousy of David.

The Song of the Bow

2SM 1:17-27

David's lament over war, in which he expresses his sorrow over the deaths of King Saul and Saul's son Jonathan.

David's Song of Thanksgiving
2SM 22

Also recorded in Psalm 18, a song that celebrates many times God delivered David from his enemies and preserved his life.

Asaph's Songs for the Temple
1CH 16:7-36;
2CH 5:13

Two songs of praise, the first sung when David commissioned the building of the temple, and the second sung when the temple was completed.

The Song of the Vineyard
IS 5:1-7

A parable song, comparing the beauty of a well-kept vineyard and its keeper to Israel and the Lord.

Ezekiel's Laments
EZK 19; 26:17-1;
27; 28:12-19

A series of laments in which the prophet Ezekiel mourns Israel's captivity and the coming judgment and ruin of Babylon.

Amos's Lament
AM 5:1-2

A dirge comparing the desolation of Israel to an abandoned virgin.

The Magnificat
LK 1:46-55

Mary's song of praise and trust after Gabriel told her she would give birth to the Messiah.

The Benedictus

LK 1:67-79

Zechariah's song of praise at the birth of John the Baptist.

The Nunc Dimittis

LK 2:28-32

The song of praise from Simeon after he held Jesus, praising the Lord for allowing him to see Israel's salvation.

The Christ Hymn

PHP 2:5-11

A possible early hymn structured around the Suffering Servant in Isaiah 53, which celebrates both the humility and glory of Christ.

The Centrality of Christ

COL 1:15-20

A possible early hymn expressing Christ's supremacy as Creator and Redeemer.

Worthy Is the Lamb

RV 5:9-14

The song of the four living creatures, twenty-four elders, and angels in the book of Revelation when the Lamb of God came to open the scroll.

The Song of Moses and the Lamb

RV 15:3-4

The last song in the Bible, sung by angels celebrating God's deliverance and His coming judgment.

Come, Thou

LONG-EXPECTED JESUS

Day 3

GENESIS 12:1-9

THE CALL OF ABRAM

¹ The LORD said to Abram:

> Go from your land,
> your relatives,
> and your father's house
> to the land that I will show you.
> ² I will make you into a great nation,
> I will bless you,
> I will make your name great,
> and you will be a blessing.
> ³ I will bless those who bless you,
> I will curse anyone who treats you with contempt,
> and all the peoples on earth
> will be blessed through you.

⁴ So Abram went, as the LORD had told him, and Lot went with him. Abram was seventy-five years old when he left Haran. ⁵ He took his wife, Sarai, his nephew Lot, all the possessions they had accumulated, and the people they had acquired in Haran, and they set out for the land of Canaan. When they came to the land of Canaan, ⁶ Abram passed through the land to the site of Shechem, at the oak of Moreh. (At that time the Canaanites were in the land.)

⁷ The LORD appeared to Abram and said, "To your offspring I will give this land." So he built an altar there to the LORD who had appeared to him. ⁸ From there he moved on to the hill country east of Bethel and pitched his tent, with Bethel on the west and Ai on the east. He built an altar to the LORD there, and he called on the name of the LORD. ⁹ Then Abram journeyed by stages to the Negev.

GENESIS 15:1-6

THE ABRAHAMIC COVENANT

¹ After these events, the word of the LORD came to Abram in a vision:

> Do not be afraid, Abram.
> I am your shield;

your reward will be very great.

² But Abram said, "Lord GOD, what can you give me, since I am childless and the heir of my house is Eliezer of Damascus?" ³ Abram continued, "Look, you have given me no offspring, so a slave born in my house will be my heir."

4 Now the word of the Lord came to him: "This one will not be your heir; instead, one who comes from your own body will be your heir." 5 He took him outside and said, "Look at the sky and count the stars, if you are able to count them." Then he said to him, "Your offspring will be that numerous."

6 Abram believed the Lord, and he credited it to him as righteousness.

GENESIS 21:1-7

THE BIRTH OF ISAAC

1 The Lord came to Sarah as he had said, and the Lord did for Sarah what he had promised. 2 Sarah became pregnant and bore a son to Abraham in his old age, at the appointed time God had told him. 3 Abraham named his son who was born to him—the one Sarah bore to him—Isaac. 4 When his son Isaac was eight days old, Abraham circumcised him, as God had commanded him. 5 Abraham was a hundred years old when his son Isaac was born to him.

6 Sarah said, "God has made me laugh, and everyone who hears will laugh with me." 7 She also said, "Who would have told Abraham that Sarah would nurse children? Yet I have borne a son for him in his old age."

PAUSE ___ *HERE* | Underline Genesis 12:3, God's blessing to one couple as the beginning of the blessing of all people.

HEBREWS 11:8-12

8 By faith Abraham, when he was called, obeyed and set out for a place that he was going to receive as an inheritance. He went out, even though he did not know where he was going. 9 By faith he stayed as a foreigner in the land of promise, living in tents as did Isaac and Jacob, coheirs of the same promise. 10 For he was looking forward to the city that has foundations, whose architect and builder is God.

11 By faith even Sarah herself, when she was unable to have children, received power to conceive offspring, even though she was past the age, since she considered that the one who had promised was faithful. 12 Therefore, from one man—in fact, from one as good as dead—came offspring as numerous as the stars of the sky and as innumerable as the grains of sand along the seashore.

/ TAKE NOTE /

38 "I speak what I have seen in the presence of the Father; so then, you do what you have heard from your father."

39 "Our father is Abraham," they replied.

"If you were Abraham's children," Jesus told them, "you would do what Abraham did. 40 But now you are trying to kill me, a man who has told you the truth that I heard from God. Abraham did not do this. 41 You're doing what your father does."

"We weren't born of sexual immorality," they said. "We have one Father—God."

42 Jesus said to them, "If God were your Father, you would love me, because I came from God and I am here. For I didn't come on my own, but he sent me. 43 Why don't you understand what I say? Because you cannot listen to my word. 44 You are of your father the devil, and you want to carry out your father's desires. He was a murderer from the beginning and does not stand in the truth, because there is no truth in him. When he tells a lie, he speaks from his own nature, because he is a liar and the father of lies. 45 Yet because I tell the truth, you do not believe me. 46 Who among you can convict me of sin? If I am telling the truth, why don't you believe me? 47 The one who is from God listens to God's words. This is why you don't listen, because you are not from God."

JESUS AND ABRAHAM

48 The Jews responded to him, "Aren't we right in saying that you're a Samaritan and have a demon?"

49 "I do not have a demon," Jesus answered. "On the contrary, I honor my Father and you dishonor me. 50 I do not seek my own glory; there is one who seeks it and judges. 51 Truly I tell you, if anyone keeps my word, he will never see death."

52 Then the Jews said, "Now we know you have a demon. Abraham died and so did the prophets. You say, 'If anyone keeps my word, he will never taste death.' 53 Are you greater than our father Abraham who died? And the prophets died. Who do you claim to be?"

54 "If I glorify myself," Jesus answered, "my glory is nothing. My Father—about whom you say, 'He is our God'—he is the one who glorifies me. 55 You do not know him, but I know him. If I were to say I don't know him, I would be a liar like you. But I do know him, and I keep his word. 56 Your father Abraham rejoiced to see my day; he saw it and was glad."

57 The Jews replied, "You aren't fifty years old yet, and you've seen Abraham?"

58 Jesus said to them, "Truly I tell you, before Abraham was, I am."

GALATIANS 3:7-9, 16-18, 27-29

7 You know, then, that those who have faith, these are Abraham's sons. 8 Now the Scripture saw in advance that God would justify the Gentiles by faith and proclaimed the gospel ahead of time to Abraham, saying, All the nations will be blessed through you. 9 Consequently, those who have faith are blessed with Abraham, who had faith.

…

16 Now the promises were spoken to Abraham and to his seed. He does not say "and to seeds," as though referring to many, but referring to one, and to your seed, who is Christ. 17 My point is this: The law, which came 430 years later, does not invalidate a covenant previously established by God and thus cancel the promise. 18 For if the inheritance is based on the law, it is no longer based on the promise; but God has graciously given it to Abraham through the promise.

…

SONS AND HEIRS

27 For those of you who were baptized into Christ have been clothed with Christ. 28 There is no Jew or Greek, slave or free, male and female; since you are all one in Christ Jesus. 29 And if you belong to Christ, then you are Abraham's seed, heirs according to the promise.

HOW DOES TODAY'S READING DESCRIBE WHAT IT MEANS THAT WE HAVE BECOME ABRAHAM'S HEIRS IN CHRIST? HOW DOES THIS REALITY INFORM THE WAY YOU CELEBRATE CHRIST'S BIRTH?

Use the space below to respond,
reflect on the reading, journal, or record a prayer.

DAY
4

Come, THOU LONG-EXPECTED JESUS

GENESIS 22:1-18

THE SACRIFICE OF ISAAC

¹ After these things God tested Abraham and said to him, "Abraham!"

"Here I am," he answered.

² "Take your son," he said, "your only son Isaac, whom you love, go to the land of Moriah, and offer him there as a burnt offering on one of the mountains I will tell you about."

³ So Abraham got up early in the morning, saddled his donkey, and took with him two of his young men and his son Isaac. He split wood for a burnt offering and set out to go to the place God had told him about. ⁴ On the third day Abraham looked up and saw the place in the distance. ⁵ Then Abraham said to his young men, "Stay here with the donkey. The boy and I will go over there to worship; then we'll come back to you." ⁶ Abraham took the wood for the burnt offering and laid it on his son Isaac. In his hand he took the fire and the knife, and the two of them walked on together.

⁷ Then Isaac spoke to his father Abraham and said, "My father."

And he replied, "Here I am, my son."

Isaac said, "The fire and the wood are here, but where is the lamb for the burnt offering?"

⁸ Abraham answered,

"God himself will provide the lamb for the burnt offering, my son."

Then the two of them walked on together.

⁹ When they arrived at the place that God had told him about, Abraham built the altar there and arranged the wood. He bound his son Isaac and placed him on the altar on top of the wood. ¹⁰ Then Abraham reached out and took the knife to slaughter his son.

¹¹ But the angel of the LORD called to him from heaven and said, "Abraham, Abraham!"

He replied, "Here I am."

¹² Then he said, "Do not lay a hand on the boy or do anything to him. For now I know that you fear God, since you have not withheld your only son from me." ¹³ Abraham looked up and saw a ram caught in the thicket by its horns. So Abraham went and took the ram and offered it as a burnt offering in place of his son. ¹⁴ And Abraham named that place The LORD Will Provide, so today it is said, "It will be provided on the LORD's mountain."

¹⁵ Then the angel of the LORD called to Abraham a second time from heaven ¹⁶ and said, "By myself I have sworn," this is the LORD's declaration: "Because you have done this thing and have not withheld your only son, ¹⁷ I will indeed bless you and make your offspring as numerous as the stars of the sky and the sand on the seashore. Your offspring will possess the city gates of their enemies. ¹⁸ And all the nations of the earth will be blessed by your offspring because you have obeyed my command."

PSALM 130

AWAITING REDEMPTION

A song of ascents.

¹ Out of the depths I call to you, LORD!
² Lord, listen to my voice;
let your ears be attentive
to my cry for help.

³ LORD, if you kept an account of iniquities,
Lord, who could stand?
⁴ But with you there is forgiveness,
so that you may be revered.

⁵ I wait for the LORD; I wait
and put my hope in his word.
⁶ I wait for the Lord
more than watchmen for the morning—
more than watchmen for the morning.

⁷ Israel, put your hope in the Lord.
For there is faithful love with the Lord,
and with him is redemption in abundance.
⁸ And he will redeem Israel
from all its iniquities.

PAUSE — HERE

Underline examples of waiting from the Old Testament reading.
Use a different color to underline moments of God's provision.

JOHN 1:29-34

THE LAMB OF GOD

²⁹ The next day John saw Jesus coming toward him and said,

"Look, the Lamb of God, who takes away the sin of the world!

³⁰ This is the one I told you about: 'After me comes a man who ranks ahead of me, because he existed before me.' ³¹ I didn't know him, but I came baptizing with water so that he might be revealed to Israel." ³² And John testified, "I saw the Spirit descending from heaven like a dove, and he rested on him. ³³ I didn't know him, but he who sent me to baptize with water told me, 'The one you see the Spirit descending and resting on—he is the one who baptizes with the Holy Spirit.' ³⁴ I have seen and testified that this is the Son of God."

JOHN 3:16-21

¹⁶ "For God loved the world in this way: He gave his one and only Son, so that everyone who believes in him will not perish but have eternal life. ¹⁷ For God did not send his Son into the world to condemn the world, but to save the world through him. ¹⁸ Anyone who believes in him is not condemned, but anyone who does not believe is already condemned, because he has not believed in the name of the one and only Son of God. ¹⁹ This is the judgment: The light has come into the world, and people loved darkness rather than the light because their deeds were evil. ²⁰ For everyone who does evil hates the light and avoids it, so that his deeds may not be exposed. ²¹ But anyone who lives by the truth comes to the light, so that his works may be shown to be accomplished by God."

HOW DOES TODAY'S NEW TESTAMENT READING
DEMONSTRATE GOD'S PROVISION?

———————

Use the space below to respond,
reflect on the reading, journal, or record a prayer.

CRAFT

COLOR BLOCK
SCARF

difficulty
MEDIUM

total time
8-12 HOURS

SUPPLIES

☐ **Super bulky (size 6) weight yarn:**

   1 (106-yard) ball of yarn in first color
   choice (referred to as color A in the
   instructions)

   2 (106-yard) balls of yarn in second color
   choice (referred to as color B in the
   instructions)

☐ **Size 15 (10-millimeter) knitting needles**

☐ **Scissors**

☐ **3½-inch square cardboard piece**

☐ **Ruler or measuring tape**

☐ **Tapestry needle**

 Scan this QR code for a PDF of the
instructions with guided steps and photos
to start making your scarf!

CRAFT

instructions

01

CASTING ON

Begin with color A, or the color that will be on the ends of the scarf. To **create a slipknot**, make a loop with the yarn and bring the yarn connected to the ball of yarn, or the "working yarn," through the loop, tightening to create another loop with a knot at the end. Slide the slipknot onto one needle and pull the excess yarn to tighten the knot. Wrap the yarn around your left finger to create a loop around. In your right hand, bring the same needle under and up through the loop and remove your finger, pulling the yarn to tighten the loop around the needle. Continue creating loops and transferring them to the needle until you have **16 loops, or stitches**, cast onto the needle.

02

KNITTING GARTER STITCH

Insert your empty needle through the first or top stitch from front to back, left to right. Make sure the working yarn is behind the right needle. Wrap the yarn counterclockwise, coming between the two needles. Slide the right needle under the left needle, catching the wrapped yarn and bringing the needle to the front. This forms the new stitch on the right needle. Slide the stitch off the left needle so the newly completed stitch is now on the right needle. Repeat these steps for each stitch on the left needle until the entire row is transferred to the right needle. Once the row is complete, the right needle becomes the left needle and the process repeats for the next row. **Knit the scarf in garter stitch until the scarf measures 4 inches in length.**

03

CHANGING COLORS

When you're ready to start **knitting in color B,** simply drop the first color and pick up the yarn for the second color, leaving a 6-inch tail. Insert your needle into the first stitch and loop the new yarn over the right needle, just as you would normally. Knit the stitch with the new color and complete the row. Trim a 6-inch tail from color A and set the remaining ball aside while you work in color B. **Continue knitting in garter stitch until the scarf measures 56 inches from the beginning. Change back to color A and continue knitting for 4 inches.**

04
BINDING
OFF

To **bind off**, or end, the scarf, knit the first 2 stitches as you would normally. Use the end of the left needle to pick up the first stitch and lift it over the second stitch and the tip of the right needle, leaving one stitch on the right needle. Knit the next stitch and repeat the process until one stitch remains on the right needle. Trim the working yarn, leaving 6 inches to weave in. Slip this last stitch off the needle and thread the 6-inch tail through the loop and pull tight, securing the yarn so the loop won't unravel. Thread the tail onto a tapestry needle and weave the yarn through some of the stitches along the edge of the scarf to hide them. Return to the areas where the scarf changes colors and **weave those ends in** along the edge to hide all yarn tails.

05
CREATE
THE TASSELS

Place the cardboard piece in front of you. **Cut a 6-inch piece** of yarn in color A and place it lengthwise along the top of your cardboard piece.

Wrap the remaining yarn 10 times around the cardboard from top to bottom, perpendicular to the 6-inch piece at the top. Leave the ball of yarn attached. Bring the ends of the 6-inch piece around the wrapped yarn and double knot the string. Leave the edges hanging over the top.

Slide the bundle off of the cardboard piece and **cut** through the end opposite the knot.

Take the working yarn from the ball and twist it around the top of your loops. Tighten it on the loops about 1 inch down. Repeat this process three times, pulling tightly each time. **Trim the working yarn** to be the length of the tassel and **knot it** to secure the bundle.

Repeat until you have the desired number of tassels for your scarf. (We made 5 for each side of the scarf, making 10 tassels total!)

06
FINISHING
THE SCARF

Attach the tassels to the scarf at desired intervals by tying the 6-inch piece of yarn from the top of the tassel to the end of your scarf. Weave the tassel's yarn ends back into the scarf with a tapestry needle.

DAY 5

COME, THOU LONG-EXPECTED JESUS,
/ BORN to SET THY PEOPLE free; /
FROM our FEARS and SINS RELEASE US;
LET US find our REST IN THEE.
ISRAEL'S STRENGTH and CONSOLATION,
HOPE OF all the earth THOU ART;
DEAR DESIRE OF ev'ry NATION,
JOY OF EV'RY longing heart.

BORN THY PEOPLE to deliver,
BORN a child, AND YET A KING,
BORN TO reign IN US FOREVER,
NOW THY GRACIOUS kingdom BRING.
BY THINE OWN ETERNAL SPIRIT rule
IN ALL OUR HEARTS alone;
BY THINE all-sufficient MERIT,
RAISE US TO THY GLORIOUS throne.

EXODUS 3:7-17

[7] Then the Lord said, "I have observed the misery of my people in Egypt, and have heard them crying out because of their oppressors. I know about their sufferings,

[8] and I have come down to rescue them

from the power of the Egyptians and to bring them from that land to a good and spacious land, a land flowing with milk and honey—the territory of the Canaanites, Hethites, Amorites, Perizzites, Hivites, and Jebusites. [9] So because the Israelites' cry for help has come to me, and I have also seen the way the Egyptians are oppressing them, [10] therefore, go. I am sending you to Pharaoh so that you may lead my people, the Israelites, out of Egypt."

[11] But Moses asked God, "Who am I that I should go to Pharaoh and that I should bring the Israelites out of Egypt?"

[12] He answered, "I will certainly be with you, and this will be the sign to you that I am the one who sent you: when you bring the people out of Egypt, you will all worship God at this mountain."

[13] Then Moses asked God, "If I go to the Israelites and say to them, 'The God of your ancestors has sent me to you,' and they ask me, 'What is his name?' what should I tell them?"

[14] God replied to Moses, "I AM WHO I AM. This is what you are to say to the Israelites: I AM has sent me to you." [15] God also said to Moses, "Say this to the Israelites: The Lord, the God of your ancestors, the God of Abraham, the God of Isaac, and the God of Jacob, has sent me to you. This is my name forever; this is how I am to be remembered in every generation.

[16] "Go and assemble the elders of Israel and say to them: The Lord, the God of your ancestors, the God of Abraham, Isaac, and Jacob, has appeared to me and said: I have paid close attention to you and to what has been done to you in Egypt. [17] And I have promised you that I will bring you up from the misery of Egypt to the land of the Canaanites, Hethites, Amorites, Perizzites, Hivites, and Jebusites—a land flowing with milk and honey."

EXODUS 6:2-11
GOD PROMISES FREEDOM

[2] Then God spoke to Moses, telling him, "I am the Lord. [3] I appeared to Abraham, Isaac, and Jacob as God Almighty, but I was not known to them by my name 'the Lord.' [4] I also established my covenant with them to give them the land of Canaan, the land they lived in as aliens. [5] Furthermore, I have heard the groaning of the Israelites, whom the Egyptians are forcing to work as slaves, and I have remembered my covenant.

[6] "Therefore tell the Israelites: I am the Lord, and I will bring you out from the forced labor of the Egyptians and rescue you from slavery to them. I will redeem you with an outstretched arm and great acts of judgment. [7] I will take you as my people, and I will be your God. You will know that I am the Lord your God, who brought you out from the forced labor of the Egyptians. [8] I will bring you to the land that I swore to give Abraham, Isaac, and Jacob, and I will give it to you as a possession. I am the Lord." [9] Moses told this to the Israelites, but they did not listen to him because of their broken spirit and hard labor.

[10] Then the Lord spoke to Moses, [11] "Go and tell Pharaoh king of Egypt to let the Israelites go from his land."

PSALM 118:1-7
THANKSGIVING FOR VICTORY

[1] Give thanks to the Lord, for he is good;
his faithful love endures forever.
[2] Let Israel say,
"His faithful love endures forever."
[3] Let the house of Aaron say,
"His faithful love endures forever."
[4] Let those who fear the Lord say,
"His faithful love endures forever."

[5] I called to the Lord in distress;
the Lord answered me
and put me in a spacious place.
[6] The Lord is for me; I will not be afraid.
What can a mere mortal do to me?

⁷ The Lᴏʀᴅ is my helper;
therefore, I will look in triumph on those who hate me.

pause // Circle what you notice in today's Old Testament reading about God's actions for the sake of His people's freedom. //

JOHN 8:31-36

³¹ Then Jesus said to the Jews who had believed him, "If you continue in my word, you really are my disciples. ³² You will know the truth, and the truth will set you free."

³³ "We are descendants of Abraham," they answered him, "and we have never been enslaved to anyone. How can you say, 'You will become free'?"

³⁴ Jesus responded, "Truly I tell you, everyone who commits sin is a slave of sin. ³⁵ A slave does not remain in the household forever, but a son does remain forever. ³⁶ So if the Son sets you free, you really will be free."

HEBREWS 3:1-6

OUR APOSTLE AND HIGH PRIEST

¹ Therefore, holy brothers and sisters, who share in a heavenly calling, consider Jesus, the apostle and high priest of our confession. ² He was faithful to the one who appointed him, just as Moses was in all God's household. ³ For Jesus is considered worthy of more glory than Moses, just as the builder has more honor than the house. ⁴ Now every house is built by someone, but the one who built everything is God. ⁵ Moses was faithful as a servant in all God's household, as a testimony to what would be said in the future. ⁶ But Christ was faithful as a Son over his household. And we are that household if we hold on to our confidence and the hope in which we boast.

GALATIANS 5:1

For freedom, Christ set us free. Stand firm, then, and don't submit again to a yoke of slavery.

HOW IS TODAY'S NEW TESTAMENT READING A REMINDER THAT GOD CAME DOWN TO RESCUE US FULLY IN THE PERSON OF JESUS?

———————

Use the space below to respond,
reflect on the reading, journal, or record a prayer.

BORN TO SET
THY PEOPLE FREE

DAY 6

ISAIAH 49:8-12

[8] This is what the LORD says:

I will answer you in a time of favor,
and I will help you in the day of salvation.
I will keep you, and I will appoint you
to be a covenant for the people,
to restore the land,
to make them possess the desolate inheritances,
[9] saying to the prisoners, "Come out,"
and to those who are in darkness, "Show yourselves."
They will feed along the pathways,
and their pastures will be on all the barren heights.
[10] They will not hunger or thirst,
the scorching heat or sun will not strike them;
for their compassionate one will guide them,
and lead them to springs.
[11] I will make all my mountains into a road,
and my highways will be raised up.
[12] See, these will come from far away,
from the north and from the west,
and from the land of Sinim.

In Isaiah 49, circle what God says He will do, and draw a box around what He will do through His people.

LUKE 4:1-22

THE TEMPTATION OF JESUS

[1] Then Jesus left the Jordan, full of the Holy Spirit, and was led by the Spirit in the wilderness [2] for forty days to be tempted by the devil. He ate nothing during those days, and when they were over, he was hungry. [3] The devil said to him, "If you are the Son of God, tell this stone to become bread."

[4] But Jesus answered him, "It is written: Man must not live on bread alone."

[5] So he took him up and showed him all the kingdoms of the world in a moment of time. [6] The devil said to him, "I will give you their splendor and all this authority, because it has been given over to me, and I can give it to anyone I want. [7] If you, then, will worship me, all will be yours."

[8] And Jesus answered him, "It is written: Worship the Lord your God, and serve him only."

[9] So he took him to Jerusalem, had him stand on the pinnacle of the temple, and said to him, "If you are the Son of God, throw yourself down from here. [10] For it is written:

He will give his angels orders concerning you,
to protect you, [11] and
they will support you with their hands,
so that you will not strike
your foot against a stone."

[12] And Jesus answered him, "It is said: Do not test the Lord your God."

[13] After the devil had finished every temptation, he departed from him for a time.

MINISTRY IN GALILEE

[14] Then Jesus returned to Galilee in the power of the Spirit, and news about him spread throughout the entire vicinity. [15] He was teaching in their synagogues, being praised by everyone.

REJECTION AT NAZARETH

[16] He came to Nazareth, where he had been brought up. As usual, he entered the synagogue on the Sabbath day and stood up to read. [17] The scroll of the prophet Isaiah was given to him, and unrolling the scroll, he found the place where it was written:

[18] The Spirit of the Lord is on me,
because he has anointed me
to preach good news to the poor.
He has sent me
to proclaim release to the captives
and recovery of sight to the blind,
to set free the oppressed,
[19] to proclaim the year of the Lord's favor.

[20] He then rolled up the scroll, gave it back to the attendant, and sat down. And the eyes of everyone in the synagogue

were fixed on him. ²¹ He began by saying to them, "Today as you listen, this Scripture has been fulfilled."

²² They were all speaking well of him and were amazed by the gracious words that came from his mouth; yet they said, "Isn't this Joseph's son?"

MARK 1:14-15

MINISTRY IN GALILEE

¹⁴ After John was arrested, Jesus went to Galilee, proclaiming the good news of God: ¹⁵ "The time is fulfilled, and the kingdom of God has come near. Repent and believe the good news!"

LUKE 13:10-17

HEALING A DAUGHTER OF ABRAHAM

¹⁰ As he was teaching in one of the synagogues on the Sabbath, ¹¹ a woman was there who had been disabled by a spirit for over eighteen years. She was bent over and could not straighten up at all. ¹² When Jesus saw her, he called out to her,

```
"Woman, you are free
of your disability."
```

¹³ Then he laid his hands on her, and instantly she was restored and began to glorify God.

¹⁴ But the leader of the synagogue, indignant because Jesus had healed on the Sabbath, responded by telling the crowd, "There are six days when work should be done; therefore come on those days and be healed and not on the Sabbath day."

¹⁵ But the Lord answered him and said, "Hypocrites! Doesn't each one of you untie his ox or donkey from the feeding trough on the Sabbath and lead it to water? ¹⁶ Satan has bound this woman, a daughter of Abraham, for eighteen years—shouldn't she be untied from this bondage on the Sabbath day?"

¹⁷ When he had said these things, all his adversaries were humiliated, but the whole crowd was rejoicing over all the glorious things he was doing.

2 CORINTHIANS 3:17

Now the Lord is the Spirit, and where the Spirit of the Lord is, there is freedom.

HEBREWS 4:14-16

OUR GREAT HIGH PRIEST

¹⁴ Therefore, since we have a great high priest who has passed through the heavens—Jesus the Son of God—let us hold fast to our confession. ¹⁵ For we do not have a high priest who is unable to sympathize with our weaknesses, but one who has been tempted in every way as we are, yet without sin. ¹⁶ Therefore, let us approach the throne of grace with boldness, so that we may receive mercy and find grace to help us in time of need.

WHAT ASPECT OF GOD'S GIFT OF FREEDOM DEMONSTRATED IN TODAY'S READING DO YOU WANT TO REFLECT ON THROUGHOUT THIS ADVENT SEASON?

Use the space below to respond,
reflect on the reading, journal, or record a prayer.

Day 7

GRACE DAY

Advent is a season to intentionally
slow our pace, contemplating and
celebrating the first coming of
Christ while also anticipating His
promised return. Take time today
to pause from the busyness of the
season to catch up on your reading,
make space for prayer, and rest in
the presence of the Lord.

Revisit "Advent Rhythms" on pages 18–19 to help reorient
your rhythms of rest and celebration.

I WAIT
for THE LORD;
I WAIT and
PUT my hope
IN HIS word.

Psalm 130:5

Day 8

THE SECOND SUNDAY

of Advent

The wilderness and the dry land will
be glad; the desert will rejoice and
blossom like a wildflower. It will
blossom abundantly and will also
rejoice with joy and singing. The
glory of Lebanon will be given to it,
the splendor of Carmel and Sharon.
They will see the glory of the LORD,
the splendor of our God.

Isaiah 35:1–2

The hymn "Lo, How a Rose E'er Blooming" combines imagery
from the Christmas story as recorded in Matthew 2 and Luke 1–2
with prophetic language from Isaiah 11:1 and 35:1–2. It also speaks
to the glorious light of Christ described in John 1. The lyrics center
the worshiper on Jesus as the stem from the root of
Jesse—the wildflower that bloomed in the wilderness.

At the heart of this lesser-known holiday tune is the reminder that
Jesus's coming was a long-awaited promise fulfilled.
What Isaiah prophesied was finally realized in the miraculous
birth of Jesus in Bethlehem.

LO, HOW A ROSE E'ER BLOOMING

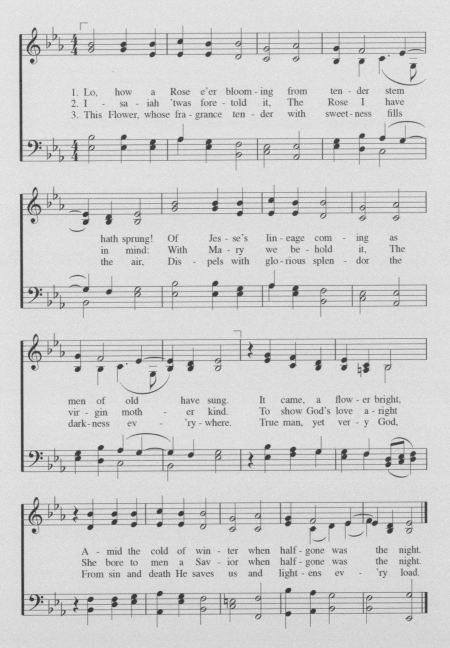

1. Lo, how a Rose e'er bloom-ing from ten-der stem
2. I - sa-iah 'twas fore-told it, The Rose I have
3. This Flower, whose fra-grance ten-der with sweet-ness fills

hath sprung! Of Jes-se's lin-eage com-ing as
in mind: With Ma-ry we be-hold it, The
the air, Dis - pels with glo-rious splen-dor the

men of old have sung. It came, a flow-er bright,
vir - gin moth - er kind. To show God's love a-right
dark-ness ev - 'ry-where. True man, yet ver-y God,

A - mid the cold of win-ter when half-gone was the night.
She bore to men a Sav-ior when half-gone was the night.
From sin and death He saves us and light-ens ev - 'ry load.

words

ORIGINAL AUTHOR UNKNOWN; STANZAS
1 AND 2 TRANSLATED BY THEODORE
BAKER; STANZA 3 TRANSLATED BY
HARRIET KRAUTH SPAETH

music

GEISTLICHE
KIRCHENGESÄNG; HARMONY
BY MICHAEL PRAETORIUS

COME, THOU LONG-EXPECTED JESUS,

BORN TO SET THY PEOPLE FREE;

FROM OUR FEARS AND SINS RELEASE US;

LET US FIND OUR REST IN THEE.

ISRAEL'S STRENGTH AND CONSOLATION,

HOPE OF ALL THE EARTH THOU ART;

DEAR DESIRE OF EV'RY NATION,

JOY OF EV'RY LONGING HEART.

BORN THY PEOPLE TO DELIVER,

BORN A CHILD, AND YET A KING,

BORN TO REIGN IN US FOREVER,

NOW THY GRACIOUS KINGDOM BRING.

BY THINE OWN ETERNAL SPIRIT RULE
IN ALL OUR HEARTS ALONE;

BY THINE ALL-SUFFICIENT MERIT,

RAISE US TO THY GLORIOUS THRONE.

PSALM 27:1-3, 7-14

MY STRONGHOLD

Of David.

1 The LORD is my light and my salvation—
whom should I fear?
The LORD is the stronghold of my life—
whom should I dread?
2 When evildoers came against me to devour my flesh,
my foes and my enemies stumbled and fell.
3 Though an army deploys against me,
my heart will not be afraid;
though a war breaks out against me,
I will still be confident.

…

7 LORD, hear my voice when I call;
be gracious to me and answer me.
8 My heart says this about you:
"Seek his face."
LORD, I will seek your face.
9 Do not hide your face from me;
do not turn your servant away in anger.
You have been my helper;
do not leave me or abandon me,
God of my salvation.
10 Even if my father and mother abandon me,
the LORD cares for me.

11 Because of my adversaries,
show me your way, LORD,
and lead me on a level path.
12 Do not give me over to the will of my foes,
for false witnesses rise up against me,
breathing violence.

13 I am certain that I will see the LORD's goodness
in the land of the living.
14 Wait for the LORD;
be strong, and let your heart be courageous.
Wait for the LORD.

PSALM 135:5-7

5 For I know that the LORD is great;
our Lord is greater than all gods.
6 The LORD does whatever he pleases
in heaven and on earth,
in the seas and all the depths.
7 He causes the clouds to rise from the ends of the earth.
He makes lightning for the rain
and brings the wind from his storehouses.

ISAIAH 43:1-3

1 Now this is what the LORD says—
the one who created you, Jacob,
and the one who formed you, Israel—
"Do not fear, for I have redeemed you;
I have called you by your name; you are mine.
2 When you pass through the waters,
I will be with you,
and the rivers will not overwhelm you.
When you walk through the fire,
you will not be scorched,
and the flame will not burn you.
3 For I am the LORD your God,
the Holy One of Israel, and your Savior.
I have given Egypt as a ransom for you,
Cush and Seba in your place."

PAUSE Underline in the Old Testament reading every reason given for not needing to fear, then continue your reading on the next page.

MATTHEW 14:22-33

[22] Immediately he made the disciples get into the boat and go ahead of him to the other side, while he dismissed the crowds. [23] After dismissing the crowds, he went up on the mountain by himself to pray. Well into the night, he was there alone. [24] Meanwhile, the boat was already some distance from land, battered by the waves, because the wind was against them. [25] Jesus came toward them walking on the sea very early in the morning. [26] When the disciples saw him walking on the sea, they were terrified. "It's a ghost!" they said, and they cried out in fear.

[27] Immediately Jesus spoke to them. "Have courage! It is I. Don't be afraid."

[28] "Lord, if it's you," Peter answered him, "command me to come to you on the water."

[29] He said, "Come."

And climbing out of the boat, Peter started walking on the water and came toward Jesus. [30] But when he saw the strength of the wind, he was afraid, and beginning to sink he cried out, "Lord, save me!"

[31] Immediately Jesus reached out his hand, caught hold of him, and said to him, "You of little faith, why did you doubt?"

[32] When they got into the boat, the wind ceased. [33] Then those in the boat worshiped him and said, "Truly you are the Son of God."

ROMANS 8:31-39

[31] What, then, are we to say about these things? If God is for us, who is against us? [32] He did not even spare his own Son but gave him up for us all. How will he not also with him grant us everything? [33] Who can bring an accusation against God's elect? God is the one who justifies. [34] Who is the one who condemns? Christ Jesus is the one who died, but even more, has been raised; he also is at the right hand of God and intercedes for us.

[35] Who can separate us from the love of Christ?

Can affliction or distress or persecution or famine or nakedness or danger or sword? [36] As it is written:

Because of you
we are being put to death all day long;
we are counted as sheep to be slaughtered.

[37] No, in all these things we are more than conquerors through him who loved us. [38] For I am persuaded that neither death nor life, nor angels nor rulers, nor things present nor things to come, nor powers, [39] nor height nor depth, nor any other created thing will be able to separate us from the love of God that is in Christ Jesus our Lord.

2 TIMOTHY 1:7

For God has not given us a spirit of fear, but one of power, love, and sound judgment.

**HOW DOES TODAY'S NEW TESTAMENT READING ENCOURAGE
YOU TO FIND COMFORT IN CHRIST WHEN YOU EXPERIENCE
FEAR? HOW CAN YOU INTENTIONALLY SEEK GOD'S COMFORT
IN YOUR ADVENT RHYTHMS?**

———————

Use the space below to respond,
reflect on the reading, journal, or record a prayer.

From Our Fears and Sins

/ RELEASE US /

Day 10

PSALM 74:10-14

[10] God, how long will the enemy mock?
Will the foe insult your name forever?
[11] Why do you hold back your hand?
Stretch out your right hand and destroy them!

[12] God my King is from ancient times,
performing saving acts on the earth.
[13] You divided the sea with your strength;
you smashed the heads of the sea monsters in the water;
[14] you crushed the heads of Leviathan;
you fed him to the creatures of the desert.

ISAIAH 25:6-9

[6] On this mountain,
the LORD of Armies will prepare for all the peoples
    a feast of choice meat,
a feast with aged wine, prime cuts of choice meat,
    fine vintage wine.
[7] On this mountain
he will swallow up the burial shroud,
the shroud over all the peoples,
the sheet covering all the nations.
[8] When he has swallowed up death once and for all,
the Lord GOD will wipe away the tears
from every face
and remove his people's disgrace
from the whole earth,
for the LORD has spoken.

[9] On that day it will be said,
"Look, this is our God;
we have waited for him, and he has saved us.
This is the LORD; we have waited for him.
Let's rejoice and be glad in his salvation."

PAUSE Underline Psalm 74:10–11, the psalmist's desire for God to destroy his enemy. PAUSE

JOHN 12:23-32

[23] Jesus replied to them, "The hour has come for the Son of Man to be glorified. [24] Truly I tell you, unless a grain of wheat falls to the ground and dies, it remains by itself. But if it dies, it produces much fruit. [25] The one who loves his life will lose it, and the one who hates his life in this world will keep it for eternal life. [26] If anyone serves me, he must follow me. Where I am, there my servant also will be. If anyone serves me, the Father will honor him.

[27] "Now my soul is troubled. What should I say—Father, save me from this hour? But that is why I came to this hour. [28] Father, glorify your name."

Then a voice came from heaven: "I have glorified it, and I will glorify it again."

[29] The crowd standing there heard it and said it was thunder. Others said, "An angel has spoken to him."

[30] Jesus responded, "This voice came, not for me, but for you. [31] Now is the judgment of this world. Now the ruler of this world will be cast out. [32] As for me, if I am lifted up from the earth I will draw all people to myself."

COLOSSIANS 2:8-15

[8] Be careful that no one takes you captive through philosophy and empty deceit based on human tradition, based on the elements of the world, rather than Christ. [9] For the entire fullness of God's nature dwells bodily in Christ, [10] and you have been filled by him, who is the head over every ruler and authority. [11] You were also circumcised in him with a circumcision not done with hands, by putting off the body of flesh, in the circumcision of Christ, [12] when you were buried with him in baptism, in which you were also raised with him through faith in the working of God, who raised him from the dead. [13] And when you were dead in trespasses and in the uncircumcision of your flesh, he made you alive with him and forgave us all our trespasses. [14] He erased the certificate of debt, with its obligations, that was against us and opposed to us, and has taken it away by nailing it to the cross. [15] He disarmed the rulers and authorities and disgraced them publicly; he triumphed over them in him.

HEBREWS 2:9-18

⁹ But we do see Jesus—made lower than the angels for a short time so that by God's grace he might taste death for everyone—crowned with glory and honor because he suffered death.

¹⁰ For in bringing many sons and daughters to glory, it was entirely appropriate that God—for whom and through whom all things exist—should make the pioneer of their salvation perfect through sufferings. ¹¹ For the one who sanctifies and those who are sanctified all have one Father. That is why Jesus is not ashamed to call them brothers and sisters, ¹² saying:

> I will proclaim your name to my brothers and sisters;
> I will sing hymns to you in the congregation.

¹³ Again, I will trust in him. And again, Here I am with the children God gave me.

¹⁴ Now since the children have flesh and blood in common, Jesus also shared in these, so that through his death he might destroy the one holding the power of death—that is, the devil— ¹⁵ and free those who were held in slavery all their lives by the fear of death. ¹⁶ For it is clear that he does not reach out to help angels, but to help Abraham's offspring. ¹⁷ Therefore, he had to be like his brothers and sisters in every way, so that he could become a merciful and faithful high priest in matters pertaining to God, to make atonement for the sins of the people. ¹⁸ For since he himself has suffered when he was tempted, he is able to help those who are tempted.

ACTS 5:29-32

²⁹ Peter and the apostles replied, "We must obey God rather than people. ³⁰ The God of our ancestors raised up Jesus, whom you had murdered by hanging him on a tree. ³¹ God exalted this man to his right hand as ruler and Savior, to give repentance to Israel and forgiveness of sins. ³² We are witnesses of these things, and so is the Holy Spirit whom God has given to those who obey him."

ACTS 26:17-18

¹⁷ "I will rescue you from your people and from the Gentiles. I am sending you to them ¹⁸ to open their eyes so that they may turn from darkness to light and from the power of Satan to God, that they may receive forgiveness of sins and a share among those who are sanctified by faith in me."

**ACCORDING TO TODAY'S READING,
HOW DID GOD BECOMING MAN FREE US FROM SIN,
DEATH, AND THE ENEMY?**

———————

Use the space below to respond,
reflect on the reading, journal, or record a prayer.

THE TRINITY

During Advent, we anticipate and prepare to celebrate the birth of Jesus. But Christmas Day was not the beginning of humanity's relationship with God. Our God is three persons—God the Father, the Son, and the Holy Spirit—yet still one God.

The Advent season is a reflection on the wonderful reality of the *incarnation*, when God took on human nature and flesh. In Jesus, we find the embodiment of God, the Son who is both fully God and fully human. Since the earliest days of the Church, believers have sought to put into words the reality of the Trinity. On the following pages you will find an excerpt from the Athanasian Creed, one of the most widely-accepted statements about the Trinity, along with key texts from Scripture.

We worship one God in trinity and the trinity in unity,
neither blending their persons
nor dividing their essence.
　For the person of the Father is a distinct person,
　the person of the Son is another,
　and that of the Holy Spirit is still another.
　But the divinity of the Father, Son, and Holy Spirit is one,
　their glory equal, their majesty coeternal.

What quality the Father has, the Son has,
　and the Holy Spirit has.
　The Father is uncreated,
　the Son is uncreated,
　the Holy Spirit is uncreated.

　The Father is immeasurable,
　the Son is immeasurable,
　the Holy Spirit is immeasurable.

　The Father is eternal,
　the Son is eternal,
　the Holy Spirit is eternal.

　　And yet there are not three eternal beings;
　　there is but one eternal being.
　　So too there are not three uncreated
　　　or immeasurable beings;
　　there is but one uncreated and immeasurable being.
...

The Father was neither made nor created nor
　begotten from anyone.
The Son was neither made nor created;
He was begotten from the Father alone.
The Holy Spirit was neither made nor created
　nor begotten;
He proceeds from the Father and the Son.

...

THE TRINITY, CONTINUED

EXCERPT FROM THE ATHANASIAN CREED

Nothing in this trinity is before or after,
nothing is greater or smaller;
in their entirety the three persons
are coeternal and coequal with each other.

So in everything, as was said earlier,
we must worship their trinity in their unity
and their unity in their trinity.

...

But it is necessary for eternal salvation
that one also believe in the incarnation
of our Lord Jesus Christ faithfully.

Now this is the true faith:

That we believe and confess
that our Lord Jesus Christ, God's Son,
is both God and human, equally.

He is God from the essence of the Father,
begotten before time;
and he is human from the essence of his mother,
born in time;
completely God, completely human,
with a rational soul and human flesh;
equal to the Father as regards divinity,
less than the Father as regards humanity.

Although he is God and human,
yet Christ is not two, but one.
He is one, however,
not by his divinity being turned into flesh,
but by God's taking humanity to himself.
He is one,
certainly not by the blending of his essence,
but by the unity of his person.
For just as one human is both rational soul and flesh,
so too the one Christ is both God and human.

KEY SCRIPTURES

Matthew 3:16–17

John 1:1–3

2 Corinthians 13:13

Hebrews 1:2–3

1 Peter 1:1–2

Jude 20–21

FROM OUR FEARS
AND SINS RELEASE US

DAY 11

ISAIAH 53

[1] Who has believed what we have heard?
And to whom has the arm of the LORD been revealed?
[2] He grew up before him like a young plant
and like a root out of dry ground.
He didn't have an impressive form
or majesty that we should look at him,
no appearance that we should desire him.
[3] He was despised and rejected by men,
a man of suffering who knew what sickness was.
He was like someone people turned away from;
he was despised, and we didn't value him.

[4] Yet he himself bore our sicknesses,
and he carried our pains;
but we in turn regarded him stricken,
struck down by God, and afflicted.

[5] But he was pierced because of our rebellion,
crushed because of our iniquities;

punishment for our peace was on him,
and we are healed by his wounds.
[6] We all went astray like sheep;
we all have turned to our own way;
and the LORD has punished him
for the iniquity of us all.

[7] He was oppressed and afflicted,
yet he did not open his mouth.
Like a lamb led to the slaughter
and like a sheep silent before her shearers,
he did not open his mouth.
[8] He was taken away because of oppression and judgment,
and who considered his fate?
For he was cut off from the land of the living;
he was struck because of my people's rebellion.
[9] He was assigned a grave with the wicked,
but he was with a rich man at his death,
because he had done no violence
and had not spoken deceitfully.

[10] Yet the LORD was pleased to crush him severely.
When you make him a guilt offering,
he will see his seed, he will prolong his days,
and by his hand, the LORD's pleasure will be accomplished.

TAKE NOTE

¹¹ After his anguish,
he will see light and be satisfied.
By his knowledge,
my righteous servant will justify many,
and he will carry their iniquities.
¹² Therefore I will give him the many as a portion,
and he will receive the mighty as spoil,
because he willingly submitted to death,
and was counted among the rebels;
yet he bore the sin of many
and interceded for the rebels.

> **PAUSE** In today's Old Testament reading underline the prophecies about what this servant would do for God's people. **PAUSE**

2 CORINTHIANS 5:21

He made the one who did not know sin to be sin for us, so that in him we might become the righteousness of God.

ROMANS 6:1-14

THE NEW LIFE IN CHRIST

¹ What should we say then? Should we continue in sin so that grace may multiply? ² Absolutely not! How can we who died to sin still live in it? ³ Or are you unaware that all of us who were baptized into Christ Jesus were baptized into his death? ⁴ Therefore we were buried with him by baptism into death, in order that, just as Christ was raised from the dead by the glory of the Father, so we too may walk in newness of life. ⁵ For if we have been united with him in the likeness of his death, we will certainly also be in the likeness of his resurrection. ⁶ For we know that our old self was crucified with him so that the body ruled by sin might be rendered powerless so that we may no longer be enslaved to sin, ⁷ since a person who has died is freed from sin. ⁸ Now if we died with Christ, we believe that we will also live with him, ⁹ because we know that Christ, having been raised from the dead, will not die again. Death no longer rules over him.

¹⁰ For the death he died,
he died to sin once for all time;

but the life he lives, he lives to God. ¹¹ So, you too consider yourselves dead to sin and alive to God in Christ Jesus.

¹² Therefore do not let sin reign in your mortal body, so that you obey its desires. ¹³ And do not offer any parts of it to sin as weapons for unrighteousness. But as those who are alive from the dead, offer yourselves to God, and all the parts of yourselves to God as weapons for righteousness. ¹⁴ For sin will not rule over you, because you are not under the law but under grace.

1 PETER 2:24-25

²⁴ He himself bore our sins in his body on the tree; so that, having died to sins, we might live for righteousness. By his wounds you have been healed. ²⁵ For you were like sheep going astray, but you have now returned to the Shepherd and Overseer of your souls.

HOW DOES TODAY'S NEW TESTAMENT READING INVITE YOU TO LIVE DIFFERENTLY IN RESPONSE TO THE FREEDOM FROM FEAR AND SIN THAT JESUS HAS SECURED FOR YOU?

Use the space below to respond,
reflect on the reading, journal, or record a prayer.

/ PEPPER JELLY /

prep time	*cook time*	*yields*
/ 45 MINUTES	/ 20 MINUTES	/ 6 (8-OUNCE) JARS /

INGREDIENTS

- ☐ 1 PACKAGE BACON, COOKED AND CHOPPED
- ☐ 1 (8-OUNCE) JAR DICED JALAPEÑOS
- ☐ 3 HEAPING CUPS FRESH, SEEDED, CHOPPED BELL PEPPERS (RED OR GREEN)
- ☐ 1 PACKAGE SURE-JELL® FRUIT PECTIN
- ☐ 1/2 TABLESPOON BUTTER OR MARGARINE
- ☐ 5 CUPS SUGAR
- ☐ RED OR GREEN FOOD COLORING (OPTIONAL)

DIRECTIONS

Cook bacon and set aside to drain grease. Once cooled, roughly chop bacon into small pieces.

Drain jalapeños, saving vinegar and setting aside. Place bell peppers and jalapeños in a 6-quart saucepan. Add 4 tablespoons of vinegar and stir in pectin. Add butter to reduce foaming. Bring mixture to full, rolling boil (a boil that doesn't stop bubbling when stirred) on high heat, stirring constantly. Stir in sugar and let fully dissolve. Add bacon pieces and stir. Return to full, rolling boil and boil exactly 1 minute, stirring constantly. Remove from heat. Skim off any foam with metal spoon. If wanted, add 4 to 6 drops of food coloring until you reach your desired shade.

Ladle immediately into jars, filling within ¼ inch from the top.

Make sure to refrigerate jelly. Jelly is good for up to one month.

· **HELPFUL TIP** · IF YOU HAVE EXPERIENCE WITH CANNING, THIS RECIPE CAN BE ADAPTED TO MAKE A PRESERVED JELLY.

LET US FIND OUR
REST IN THEE

DAY 12

EXODUS 33:12-14

THE LORD'S GLORY

¹² Moses said to the LORD, "Look, you have told me, 'Lead this people up,' but you have not let me know whom you will send with me. You said, 'I know you by name, and you have also found favor with me.' ¹³ Now if I have indeed found favor with you, please teach me your ways, and I will know you, so that I may find favor with you. Now consider that this nation is your people."

¹⁴ And he replied, "My presence will go with you, and I will give you rest."

PSALM 23:1-3

THE GOOD SHEPHERD

A psalm of David.

¹ The LORD is my shepherd;
I have what I need.

² He lets me lie down in green pastures;
he leads me beside quiet waters.

³ He renews my life;
he leads me along the right paths
for his name's sake.

PSALM 62:1-2

TRUST IN GOD ALONE

For the choir director: according to Jeduthun. A psalm of David.

¹ I am at rest in God alone;
my salvation comes from him.
² He alone is my rock and my salvation,
my stronghold; I will never be shaken.

ISAIAH 40:28-31

²⁸ Do you not know?
Have you not heard?
The LORD is the everlasting God,
the Creator of the whole earth.
He never becomes faint or weary;
there is no limit to his understanding.

/ TAKE NOTE /

²⁹ He gives strength to the faint
and strengthens the powerless.
³⁰ Youths may become faint and weary,
and young men stumble and fall,
³¹ but those who trust in the LORD
will renew their strength;
they will soar on wings like eagles;
they will run and not become weary,
they will walk and not faint.

 PAUSE HERE Circle the images of rest in the Old Testament reading that caught your attention.

JOHN 10:7-30

⁷ Jesus said again, "Truly I tell you, I am the gate for the sheep. ⁸ All who came before me are thieves and robbers, but the sheep didn't listen to them. ⁹ I am the gate. If anyone enters by me, he will be saved and will come in and go out and find pasture. ¹⁰ A thief comes only to steal and kill and destroy. I have come so that they may have life and have it in abundance.

¹¹ "I am the good shepherd. The good shepherd lays down his life for the sheep. ¹² The hired hand, since he is not the shepherd and doesn't own the sheep, leaves them and runs away when he sees a wolf coming. The wolf then snatches and scatters them. ¹³ This happens because he is a hired hand and doesn't care about the sheep.

¹⁴ "I am the good shepherd. I know my own, and my own know me, ¹⁵ just as the Father knows me, and I know the Father. I lay down my life for the sheep. ¹⁶ But I have other sheep that are not from this sheep pen; I must bring them also, and they will listen to my voice. Then there will be one flock, one shepherd. ¹⁷ This is why the Father loves me, because I lay down my life so that I may take it up again. ¹⁸ No one takes it from me, but I lay it down on my own. I have the right to lay it down, and I have the right to take it up again. I have received this command from my Father."

¹⁹ Again the Jews were divided because of these words. ²⁰ Many of them were saying, "He has a demon and he's crazy. Why do you listen to him?" ²¹ Others were saying, "These aren't the words of someone who is demon-possessed. Can a demon open the eyes of the blind?"

JESUS AT THE FESTIVAL OF DEDICATION

²² Then the Festival of Dedication took place in Jerusalem, and it was winter. ²³ Jesus was walking in the temple in Solomon's Colonnade. ²⁴ The Jews surrounded him and asked, "How long are you going to keep us in suspense? If you are the Messiah, tell us plainly."

²⁵ "I did tell you and you don't believe," Jesus answered them. "The works that I do in my Father's name testify about me. ²⁶ But you don't believe because you are not of my sheep. ²⁷ My sheep hear my voice, I know them, and they follow me. ²⁸ I give them eternal life, and they will never perish. No one will snatch them out of my hand. ²⁹ My Father, who has given them to me, is greater than all. No one is able to snatch them out of the Father's hand. ³⁰ I and the Father are one."

MATTHEW 11:28-30

²⁸ "Come to me, all of you who are weary and burdened, and I will give you rest. ²⁹ Take up my yoke and learn from me, because I am lowly and humble in heart, and you will find rest for your souls. ³⁰ For my yoke is easy and my burden is light."

DO THESE NEW TESTAMENT IMAGES OF RESTING IN CHRIST DESCRIBE YOUR EXPERIENCE OF THE ADVENT SEASON SO FAR? WHAT IS A PRACTICAL STEP YOU CAN TAKE TO FIND REST IN JESUS TODAY?

Use the space below to respond,
reflect on the reading, journal, or record a prayer.

COME, THOU LONG-EXPECTED JESUS,

BORN TO SET THY PEOPLE FREE;

FROM OUR FEARS AND SINS RELEASE US;

LET US FIND OUR REST IN THEE.

ISRAEL'S STRENGTH AND CONSOLATION,

HOPE OF ALL THE EARTH THOU ART;

DEAR DESIRE OF EV'RY NATION,

JOY OF EV'RY LONGING HEART.

BORN THY PEOPLE TO DELIVER,

BORN A CHILD, AND YET A KING,

BORN TO REIGN IN US FOREVER,

NOW THY GRACIOUS KINGDOM BRING.

BY THINE OWN ETERNAL SPIRIT RULE
IN ALL OUR HEARTS ALONE;

BY THINE ALL-SUFFICIENT MERIT,

RAISE US TO THY GLORIOUS THRONE.

EXODUS 15:1-3

ISRAEL'S SONG

¹ Then Moses and the Israelites sang this song to the LORD. They said:

> I will sing to the LORD,
> for he is highly exalted;
> he has thrown the horse
> and its rider into the sea.
> ² The LORD is my strength and my song;
> he has become my salvation.
> This is my God, and I will praise him,
> my father's God, and I will exalt him.
> ³ The LORD is a warrior;
> the LORD is his name.

PSALM 68:34-35

³⁴ Ascribe power to God.
His majesty is over Israel;
his power is among the clouds.
³⁵ God, you are awe-inspiring in your sanctuaries.
The God of Israel gives power and strength to his people.
Blessed be God!

pause // Underline Exodus 15:2 and Psalm 68:35, descriptions of God's salvation as a source of strength. //

LUKE 24:44-49

⁴⁴ He told them, "These are my words that I spoke to you while I was still with you—that everything written about me in the Law of Moses, the Prophets, and the Psalms must be fulfilled." ⁴⁵ Then he opened their minds to understand the Scriptures. ⁴⁶ He also said to them, "This is what is written: The Messiah will suffer and rise from the dead the third day, ⁴⁷ and repentance for forgiveness of sins will be proclaimed in his name to all the nations, beginning at Jerusalem. ⁴⁸ You are witnesses of these things. ⁴⁹ And look, I am sending you what my Father promised. As for you, stay in the city until you are empowered from on high."

JOHN 16:28-33

²⁸ "I came from the Father and have come into the world. Again, I am leaving the world and going to the Father."

[29] His disciples said, "Look, now you're speaking plainly and not using any figurative language. [30] Now we know that you know everything and don't need anyone to question you. By this we believe that you came from God."

[31] Jesus responded to them, "Do you now believe? [32] Indeed, an hour is coming, and has come, when each of you will be scattered to his own home, and you will leave me alone. Yet I am not alone, because the Father is with me. [33] I have told you these things so that in me you may have peace. You will have suffering in this world. Be courageous! I have conquered the world."

2 CORINTHIANS 12:6-10

[6] For if I want to boast, I wouldn't be a fool, because I would be telling the truth. But I will spare you, so that no one can credit me with something beyond what he sees in me or hears from me, [7] especially because of the extraordinary revelations. Therefore, so that I would not exalt myself, a thorn in the flesh was given to me, a messenger of Satan to torment me so that I would not exalt myself. [8] Concerning this, I pleaded with the Lord three times that it would leave me. [9] But he said to me, "My grace is sufficient for you, for my power is perfected in weakness."

Therefore, I will most gladly boast all the more about my weaknesses, so that Christ's power may reside in me. [10] So I take pleasure in weaknesses, insults, hardships, persecutions, and in difficulties, for the sake of Christ. For when I am weak, then I am strong.

EPHESIANS 6:10-18
CHRISTIAN WARFARE

[10] Finally, be strengthened by the Lord and by his vast strength.

[11] Put on the full armor of God so that you can stand against the schemes of the devil. [12] For our struggle is not against flesh and blood, but against the rulers, against the authorities, against the cosmic powers of this darkness, against evil, spiritual forces in the heavens. [13] For this reason take up the full armor of God, so that you may be able to resist in the evil day, and having prepared everything, to take your stand. [14] Stand, therefore, with truth like a belt around your waist, righteousness like armor on your chest, [15] and your feet sandaled with readiness for the gospel of peace. [16] In every situation take up the shield of faith with which you can extinguish all the flaming arrows of the evil one. [17] Take the helmet of salvation and the sword of the Spirit—which is the word of God. [18] Pray at all times in the Spirit with every prayer and request, and stay alert with all perseverance and intercession for all the saints.

PHILIPPIANS 4:4-14

[4] Rejoice in the Lord always. I will say it again: Rejoice! [5] Let your graciousness be known to everyone. The Lord is near. [6] Don't worry about anything, but in everything, through prayer and petition with thanksgiving, present your requests to God. [7] And the peace of God, which surpasses all understanding, will guard your hearts and minds in Christ Jesus.

[8] Finally brothers and sisters, whatever is true, whatever is honorable, whatever is just, whatever is pure, whatever is lovely, whatever is commendable—if there is any moral excellence and if there is anything praiseworthy—dwell on these things. [9] Do what you have learned and received and heard from me, and seen in me, and the God of peace will be with you.

APPRECIATION OF SUPPORT

[10] I rejoiced in the Lord greatly because once again you renewed your care for me. You were, in fact, concerned about me but lacked the opportunity to show it. [11] I don't say this out of need, for I have learned to be content in whatever circumstances I find myself. [12] I know how to make do with little, and I know how to make do with a lot. In any and all circumstances I have learned the secret of being content—whether well fed or hungry, whether in abundance or in need. [13] I am able to do all things through him who strengthens me. [14] Still, you did well by partnering with me in my hardship.

ACCORDING TO TODAY'S NEW TESTAMENT READING, HOW DOES GOD STRENGTHEN US IN CHRIST? HOW CAN WE RELY ON HIS STRENGTH AS WE ANTICIPATE HIS SECOND ADVENT?

———————

Use the space below to respond,
reflect on the reading, journal, or record a prayer.

"

THE ADVENT SEASON IS
A SEASON OF WAITING,
BUT OUR WHOLE LIFE IS
AN ADVENT SEASON, THAT
IS, A SEASON OF WAITING
FOR THE LAST ADVENT,
FOR THE TIME WHEN THERE
WILL BE A NEW HEAVEN
AND A NEW EARTH.

dietrich
BONHOEFFER

Day 14

GRACE DAY

Advent is a season to intentionally slow our pace, contemplating and celebrating the first coming of Christ while also anticipating His promised return. Take time today to pause from the busyness of the season to catch up on your reading, make space for prayer, and rest in the presence of the Lord.

Revisit "Advent Rhythms" on pages 18–19 to help reorient your rhythms of rest and celebration.

ON THAT day
IT WILL be SAID,
"LOOK, THIS IS OUR
GOD; we have WAITED
FOR HIM, and HE HAS
SAVED US. THIS IS
THE LORD; WE have
waited FOR HIM.
LET'S rejoice AND
be glad IN HIS
SALVATION."

Isaiah 25:9

Day 15

THE THIRD SUNDAY

of Advent

```
I will declare the LORD's decree.
He said to me, "You are my Son;
today I have become your Father."
```

Psalm 2:7

"Of the Father's Love Begotten" proclaims the identity and nature of Jesus Christ. Written in the fourth century by Aurelius Clemens Prudentis, this work was originally a poem inspired by theological reflections from Prudentis's personal journey of faith.

Early in the fourth century at the First Council of Nicea, the Church responded to heretical teachings about the nature of Christ by drafting The Nicene Creed. The creed declares that Christ is "begotten, not made, of one being with the Father." "Of the Father's Love Begotten" echoes the testimony of Scripture that Christ has always been God.

During the Advent season we focus on God's taking on humanity, and this centuries-old hymn offers believers a chance to sing and declare the divinity of the Son.

OF THE FATHER'S LOVE BEGOTTEN

words

AURELIUS CLEMENS PRUDENTIS;
STANZAS 1 THROUGH 4 TRANSLATED
BY JOHN MASON NEALE

music

AURELIUS CLEMENS
PRUDENTIS

ISRAEL'S STRENGTH
AND CONSOLATION

DAY 16

ISAIAH 40:1-2

GOD'S PEOPLE COMFORTED

¹ "Comfort, comfort my people,"
says your God.
² "Speak tenderly to Jerusalem,
and announce to her
that her time of hard service is over,
her iniquity has been pardoned,
and she has received from the LORD's hand
double for all her sins."

ISAIAH 49:13

Shout for joy, you heavens!
Earth, rejoice!
Mountains break into joyful shouts!
For the LORD has comforted his people,
and will have compassion on his afflicted ones.

ISAIAH 61:1-3

MESSIAH'S JUBILEE

¹ The Spirit of the Lord GOD is on me,
because the LORD has anointed me
to bring good news to the poor.
He has sent me to heal the brokenhearted,
to proclaim liberty to the captives
and freedom to the prisoners;
² to proclaim the year of the LORD's favor,
and the day of our God's vengeance;
to comfort all who mourn,
³ to provide for those who mourn in Zion;
to give them a crown of beauty instead of ashes,
festive oil instead of mourning,
and splendid clothes instead of despair.
And they will be called righteous trees,
planted by the LORD
to glorify him.

PAUSE

HERE

Underline the descriptions of
God's comfort in the Old Testament
reading, then continue your
reading on the next page.

/ TAKE NOTE /

LUKE 2:21-38

THE CIRCUMCISION AND PRESENTATION OF JESUS

[21] When the eight days were completed for his circumcision, he was named Jesus—the name given by the angel before he was conceived. [22] And when the days of their purification according to the law of Moses were finished, they brought him up to Jerusalem to present him to the Lord [23] (just as it is written in the law of the Lord, Every firstborn male will be dedicated to the Lord) [24] and to offer a sacrifice (according to what is stated in the law of the Lord, a pair of turtledoves or two young pigeons).

SIMEON'S PROPHETIC PRAISE

[25] There was a man in Jerusalem whose name was Simeon. This man was righteous and devout, looking forward to Israel's consolation, and the Holy Spirit was on him. [26] It had been revealed to him by the Holy Spirit that he would not see death before he saw the Lord's Messiah. [27] Guided by the Spirit, he entered the temple. When the parents brought in the child Jesus to perform for him what was customary under the law, [28] Simeon took him up in his arms, praised God, and said,

[29] Now, Master,
you can dismiss your servant in peace,
as you promised.
[30] For my eyes have seen your salvation.
[31] You have prepared it
in the presence of all peoples—
[32] a light for revelation to the Gentiles
and glory to your people Israel.

[33] His father and mother were amazed at what was being said about him. [34] Then Simeon blessed them and told his mother Mary, "Indeed, this child is destined to cause the fall and rise of many in Israel and to be a sign that will be opposed— [35] and a sword will pierce your own soul—that the thoughts of many hearts may be revealed."

ANNA'S TESTIMONY

[36] There was also a prophetess, Anna, a daughter of Phanuel, of the tribe of Asher. She was well along in years, having lived with her husband seven years after her marriage, [37] and was a widow for eighty-four years. She did not leave the temple, serving God night and day with fasting and prayers. [38] At that very moment, she came up and began to thank God and to speak about him to all who were looking forward to the redemption of Jerusalem.

MATTHEW 5:3-10

THE BEATITUDES

[3] "Blessed are the poor in spirit,
for the kingdom of heaven is theirs.
[4] Blessed are those who mourn,
for they will be comforted.
[5] Blessed are the humble,
for they will inherit the earth.
[6] Blessed are those who hunger and thirst for righteousness,
for they will be filled.
[7] Blessed are the merciful,
for they will be shown mercy.
[8] Blessed are the pure in heart,
for they will see God.
[9] Blessed are the peacemakers,
for they will be called sons of God.
[10] Blessed are those who are persecuted because
    of righteousness,
for the kingdom of heaven is theirs."

MATTHEW 23:37

JESUS'S LAMENTING OVER JERUSALEM

"Jerusalem, Jerusalem, who kills the prophets and stones those who are sent to her. How often I wanted to gather your children together, as a hen gathers her chicks under her wings, but you were not willing!"

WHAT WERE ANNA AND SIMEON CELEBRATING WHEN THEY ENCOUNTERED THE INFANT JESUS? HOW DOES THEIR CELEBRATION REFLECT THE ANTICIPATION OF THE ADVENT SEASON?

Use the space below to respond,
reflect on the reading, journal, or record a prayer.

A GIFT GUIDE FROM 1902

There's something special about giving and receiving gifts at Christmastime. Expressed in various ways across traditions, gift giving has been a part of the Advent experience for centuries. Just as the way people practice giving gifts has changed over the years, so have the gifts! Here are a few items from the holiday gift guide in a 1902 issue of *The Ladies' Home Journal*.

GRANDMOTHER

SIDE COMBS

GOLD THIMBLE

LACE COLLAR

SIX-YEAR-OLD BOY

SOME RABBITS

HOOP AND STICKS

SLED

FATHER

GOOD ALMANAC

SHAVING MIRROR

PAPER CUTTER

GRANDFATHER

SILVER KEY CHAIN

HOUSECOAT

MAGNIFYING GLASS

MOTHER

HEMSTITCHED
HANDKERCHIEFS

COLLARS AND CUFFS

FEATHER BOA

TWELVE-YEAR-OLD BOY

BOX OF PAINTS

LANTERN

PUNCHING BAG

LITTLE GIRL

PAPER DOLLS

TENNIS RACKET

PARTY DRESS

ELDER SISTER

SILK PETTICOAT

VINAIGRETTE

SHOE BUCKLES

BABY

LACE BIB

SILVER RATTLE

RAG DOLL

DAY 17

COME, THOU LONG-EXPECTED JESUS,
BORN TO SET THY PEOPLE FREE;
FROM OUR FEARS AND SINS RELEASE US;
LET US FIND OUR REST IN THEE.
ISRAEL'S STRENGTH AND CONSOLATION,
/ HOPE OF ALL THE EARTH THOU ART; /
DEAR DESIRE OF EV'RY NATION,
JOY OF EV'RY LONGING HEART.

BORN THY PEOPLE TO DELIVER,
BORN A CHILD, AND YET A KING,
BORN TO REIGN IN US FOREVER,
NOW THY GRACIOUS KINGDOM BRING.
BY THINE OWN ETERNAL SPIRIT RULE
IN ALL OUR HEARTS ALONE;
BY THINE ALL-SUFFICIENT MERIT,
RAISE US TO THY GLORIOUS THRONE.

ISAIAH 65:17-25

A NEW CREATION

17 "For I will create new heavens
    and a new earth;
the past events will not be remembered
    or come to mind.

18 Then be glad and rejoice forever
in what I am creating;
for I will create Jerusalem to be a joy
and its people to be a delight.
19 I will rejoice in Jerusalem
and be glad in my people.
The sound of weeping and crying
will no longer be heard in her.
20 In her, a nursing infant will no longer live
only a few days,
or an old man not live out his days.
Indeed, the one who dies at a hundred years old
will be mourned as a young man,
and the one who misses a hundred years
will be considered cursed.
21 People will build houses and live in them;
they will plant vineyards and eat their fruit.
22 They will not build and others live in them;
they will not plant and others eat.
For my people's lives will be
like the lifetime of a tree.
My chosen ones will fully enjoy
the work of their hands.
23 They will not labor without success
or bear children destined for disaster,
for they will be a people blessed by the LORD
along with their descendants.

24 Even before they call, I will answer;
while they are still speaking, I will hear.
25 The wolf and the lamb will feed together,
and the lion will eat straw like cattle,
but the serpent's food will be dust!
They will not do what is evil or destroy
on my entire holy mountain,"
says the LORD.

EZEKIEL 34:25-31

25 "'I will make a covenant of peace with them and eliminate dangerous creatures from the land, so that they may live securely in the wilderness and sleep in the forest. 26 I will make them and the area around my hill a blessing: I will send down showers in their season; they will be showers of blessing. 27 The trees of the field will yield their fruit, and the land will yield its produce; my flock will be secure in their land. They will know that I am the LORD when I break the bars of their yoke and rescue them from the power of those who enslave them. 28 They will no longer be prey for the nations, and the wild creatures of the earth will not consume them. They will live securely, and no one will frighten them. 29 I will establish for them a place renowned for its agriculture, and they will no longer be victims of famine in the land. They will no longer endure the insults of the nations. 30 Then they will know that I, the LORD their God, am with them, and that they, the house of Israel, are my people. This is the declaration of the Lord GOD. 31 You are my flock, the human flock of my pasture, and I am your God. This is the declaration of the Lord GOD.'"

 PAUSE In the Old Testament reading, circle any descriptions of the earth that are different than what you've observed or experienced in the world today. After this, continue your reading on the next page.

JOHN 1:1–3, 14–18
PROLOGUE

¹ In the beginning was the Word, and the Word was with God, and the Word was God. ² He was with God in the beginning. ³ All things were created through him, and apart from him not one thing was created that has been created.

…

¹⁴ The Word became flesh and dwelt among us. We observed his glory, the glory as the one and only Son from the Father, full of grace and truth. ¹⁵ (John testified concerning him and exclaimed, "This was the one of whom I said, 'The one coming after me ranks ahead of me, because he existed before me.'") ¹⁶ Indeed, we have all received grace upon grace from his fullness, ¹⁷ for the law was given through Moses; grace and truth came through Jesus Christ. ¹⁸ No one has ever seen God. The one and only Son, who is himself God and is at the Father's side—he has revealed him.

ROMANS 8:18–25
FROM GROANS TO GLORY

¹⁸ For I consider that the sufferings of this present time are not worth comparing with the glory that is going to be revealed to us. ¹⁹ For the creation eagerly waits with anticipation for God's sons to be revealed. ²⁰ For the creation was subjected to futility—not willingly, but because of him who subjected it—in the hope ²¹ that the creation itself will also be set free from the bondage to decay into the glorious freedom of God's children. ²² For we know that the whole creation has been groaning together with labor pains until now. ²³ Not only that, but we ourselves who have the Spirit as the firstfruits—we also groan within ourselves, eagerly waiting for adoption, the redemption of our bodies. ²⁴ Now in this hope we were saved, but hope that is seen is not hope, because who hopes for what he sees? ²⁵ Now if we hope for what we do not see, we eagerly wait for it with patience.

2 PETER 3:10–13

¹⁰ But the day of the Lord will come like a thief on that day the heavens will pass away with a loud noise, the elements will burn and be dissolved, and the earth and the works on it will be disclosed. ¹¹ Since all these things are to be dissolved in this way, it is clear what sort of people you should be in holy conduct and godliness ¹² as you wait for the day of God and hasten its coming. Because of that day, the heavens will be dissolved with fire and the elements will melt with heat. ¹³ But based on his promise, we wait for new heavens and a new earth, where righteousness dwells.

REVELATION 22:1–5
THE SOURCE OF LIFE

¹ Then he showed me the river of the water of life, clear as crystal, flowing from the throne of God and of the Lamb ² down the middle of the city's main street. The tree of life was on each side of the river, bearing twelve kinds of fruit, producing its fruit every month. The leaves of the tree are for healing the nations, ³ and there will no longer be any curse. The throne of God and of the Lamb will be in the city, and his servants will worship him. ⁴ They will see his face, and his name will be on their foreheads. ⁵ Night will be no more; people will not need the light of a lamp or the light of the sun, because the Lord God will give them light, and they will reign forever and ever.

REVELATION 21:1–7
THE NEW CREATION

¹ Then I saw a new heaven and a new earth; for the first heaven and the first earth had passed away, and the sea was no more. ² I also saw the holy city, the new Jerusalem, coming down out of heaven from God, prepared like a bride adorned for her husband.

³ Then I heard a loud voice from the throne: Look, God's dwelling is with humanity, and he will live with them. They will be his peoples, and God himself will be with them and will be their God. ⁴ He will wipe away every tear from their eyes. Death will be no more; grief, crying, and pain will be no more, because the previous things have passed away.

⁵ Then the one seated on the throne said, "Look, I am making everything new." He also said, "Write, because these words are faithful and true." ⁶ Then he said to me, "It is done! I am the Alpha and the Omega, the beginning and the end. I will freely give to the thirsty from the spring of the water of life. ⁷ The one who conquers will inherit these things, and I will be his God, and he will be my son."

HOW DOES TODAY'S NEW TESTAMENT READING CONNECT JESUS TO THE NEW CREATION? IN WHAT AREAS DOES THE ADVENT SEASON GUIDE YOU TO LONG FOR THE NEW HEAVENS AND NEW EARTH?

Use the space below to respond,
reflect on the reading, journal, or record a prayer.

ROOM SPRAY

SUPPLIES

VARIOUS ESSENTIAL OILS

- ☐ ORANGE
- ☐ GRAPEFRUIT
- ☐ FRANKINCENSE
- ☐ CEDARWOOD
- ☐ CARDAMOM
- ☐ PEPPERMINT
- ☐ ROSEMARY
- ☐ CINNAMON

OTHER ITEMS

- ☐ 6 OUNCES WATER
- ☐ 2 OUNCES WITCH HAZEL LIQUID
- ☐ SPRAY BOTTLE
  (WE USED AN 8-OUNCE BOTTLE)
- ☐ DRIED FLOWERS (OPTIONAL)
- ☐ ROSEMARY SPRIGS (OPTIONAL)
- ☐ CINNAMON STICKS (OPTIONAL)

INSTRUCTIONS

1. Select which blend you want to create, and gather required essential oils.

2. Add water and witch hazel into bottle. Then, add in your essential oils and shake gently.

3. If desired, add flowers, rosemary, or cinnamon sticks to your bottle.

4. Spritz your new room spray and enjoy the scents of the season!

 HELPFUL TIP | WITCH HAZEL HELPS WATER AND OIL COMBINE, ALONG WITH ADDING LONGEVITY TO YOUR BLEND.

blend options

REFRESHING BLEND

12 drops orange

8 drops grapefruit

2 drops frankincense

2 drops cedarwood

4 drops cardamom

Dried flowers (optional)

COZY BLEND

16 drops peppermint

18 drops orange

6 drops rosemary

Rosemary sprig (optional)

SEASONAL BLEND

8 drops orange

4 drops cinnamon

4 drops frankincense

4 drops cardamom

Cinnamon stick (optional)

COME, THOU LONG-EXPECTED JESUS,

BORN TO SET THY PEOPLE FREE;

FROM OUR FEARS AND SINS RELEASE US;

LET US FIND OUR REST IN THEE.

ISRAEL'S STRENGTH AND CONSOLATION,

HOPE OF ALL THE EARTH THOU ART;

DEAR DESIRE OF EV'RY NATION,

JOY OF EV'RY LONGING HEART.

BORN THY PEOPLE TO DELIVER,

BORN A CHILD, AND YET A KING,

BORN TO REIGN IN US FOREVER,

NOW THY GRACIOUS KINGDOM BRING.

BY THINE OWN ETERNAL SPIRIT RULE
IN ALL OUR HEARTS ALONE;

BY THINE ALL-SUFFICIENT MERIT,

RAISE US TO THY GLORIOUS THRONE.

PSALM 67:1-7

ALL WILL PRAISE GOD

For the choir director: with stringed instruments.
A psalm. A song.

¹ May God be gracious to us and bless us;
may he make his face shine upon us   *Selah*
² so that your way may be known on earth,
your salvation among all nations.

³ Let the peoples praise you, God;
let all the peoples praise you.
⁴ Let the nations rejoice and shout for joy,
for you judge the peoples with fairness
and lead the nations on earth.   *Selah*
⁵ Let the peoples praise you, God,
let all the peoples praise you.

⁶ The earth has produced its harvest;
God, our God, blesses us.
⁷ God will bless us,
and all the ends of the earth will fear him.

ISAIAH 11:10

On that day the root of Jesse
will stand as a banner for the peoples.
The nations will look to him for guidance,
and his resting place will be glorious.

MICAH 4:1-7

THE LORD'S RULE FROM RESTORED ZION

¹ In the last days
the mountain of the LORD's house
will be established
at the top of the mountains
and will be raised above the hills.
Peoples will stream to it,
² and many nations will come and say,
"Come, let's go up to the mountain of the LORD,
to the house of the God of Jacob.
He will teach us about his ways
so we may walk in his paths."

For instruction will go out of Zion
and the word of the LORD from Jerusalem.
³ He will settle disputes among many peoples
and provide arbitration for strong nations
that are far away.
They will beat their swords into plows
and their spears into pruning knives.
Nation will not take up the sword against nation,
and they will never again train for war.
⁴ But each person will sit under his grapevine
and under his fig tree
with no one to frighten him.
For the mouth of the LORD of Armies
has spoken.
⁵ Though all the peoples walk
in the name of their own gods,
we will walk in the name of the LORD our God
forever and ever.

⁶ On that day—
    this is the LORD's declaration—
I will assemble the lame
and gather the scattered,
those I have injured.
⁷ I will make the lame into a remnant,
those far removed into a strong nation.
Then the LORD will reign over them in Mount Zion
from this time on and forever.

 *pause* // Underline the five mentions of "the nations" in today's Old Testament reading. //

JOHN 4:1-26

JESUS AND THE SAMARITAN WOMAN

¹ When Jesus learned that the Pharisees had heard he was making and baptizing more disciples than John ² (though Jesus himself was not baptizing, but his disciples were), ³ he left Judea and went again to Galilee. ⁴ He had to travel

through Samaria; ⁵ so he came to a town of Samaria called Sychar near the property that Jacob had given his son Joseph. ⁶ Jacob's well was there, and Jesus, worn out from his journey, sat down at the well. It was about noon.

⁷ A woman of Samaria came to draw water.

"Give me a drink," Jesus said to her, ⁸ because his disciples had gone into town to buy food.

⁹ "How is it that you, a Jew, ask for a drink from me, a Samaritan woman?" she asked him. For Jews do not associate with Samaritans.

¹⁰ Jesus answered, "If you knew the gift of God, and who is saying to you, 'Give me a drink,' you would ask him, and he would give you living water."

¹¹ "Sir," said the woman, "you don't even have a bucket, and the well is deep. So where do you get this 'living water'? ¹² You aren't greater than our father Jacob, are you? He gave us the well and drank from it himself, as did his sons and livestock."

¹³ Jesus said, "Everyone who drinks from this water will get thirsty again. ¹⁴ But whoever drinks from the water that I will give him will never get thirsty again. In fact, the water I will give him will become a well of water springing up in him for eternal life."

¹⁵ "Sir," the woman said to him, "give me this water so that I won't get thirsty and come here to draw water."

¹⁶ "Go call your husband," he told her, "and come back here."

¹⁷ "I don't have a husband," she answered.

"You have correctly said, 'I don't have a husband,'" Jesus said. ¹⁸ "For you've had five husbands, and the man you now have is not your husband. What you have said is true."

¹⁹ "Sir," the woman replied, "I see that you are a prophet. ²⁰ Our ancestors worshiped on this mountain, but you Jews say that the place to worship is in Jerusalem."

²¹ Jesus told her, "Believe me, woman, an hour is coming when you will worship the Father neither on this mountain nor in Jerusalem. ²² You Samaritans worship what you do not know. We worship what we do know, because salvation is from the Jews. ²³ But an hour is coming, and is now here, when the true worshipers will worship the Father in Spirit and in truth. Yes, the Father wants such people to worship him. ²⁴ God is spirit, and those who worship him must worship in Spirit and in truth."

²⁵ The woman said to him, "I know that the Messiah is coming" (who is called Christ). "When he comes, he will explain everything to us."

²⁶ Jesus told her, "I, the one speaking to you, am he."

MATTHEW 8:5-13

A CENTURION'S FAITH

⁵ When he entered Capernaum, a centurion came to him, pleading with him, ⁶ "Lord, my servant is lying at home paralyzed, in terrible agony."

⁷ He said to him, "Am I to come and heal him?"

⁸ "Lord," the centurion replied, "I am not worthy to have you come under my roof. But just say the word, and my servant will be healed. ⁹ For I too am a man under authority, having soldiers under my command. I say to this one, 'Go,' and he goes; and to another, 'Come,' and he comes; and to my servant, 'Do this!' and he does it."

¹⁰ Hearing this, Jesus was amazed and said to those following him, "Truly I tell you, I have not found anyone in Israel with so great a faith. ¹¹ I tell you that many will come from east and west to share the banquet with Abraham, Isaac, and Jacob in the kingdom of heaven. ¹² But the sons of the kingdom will be thrown into the outer darkness where there will be weeping and gnashing of teeth." ¹³ Then Jesus told the centurion, "Go. As you have believed, let it be done for you." And his servant was healed that very moment.

IN TODAY'S NEW TESTAMENT READING, HOW DOES JESUS SPECIFICALLY MEET THE NEEDS OF THE SAMARITAN WOMAN AND THE CENTURION, TWO NON-JEWISH PEOPLE? HOW HAS HE MET YOUR NEEDS?

———————

Use the space below to respond,
reflect on the reading, journal, or record a prayer.

DAY
19

DEAR

DESIRE

of ev'ry

NATION

ISAIAH 56:3-8

³ No foreigner who has joined himself to the Lord
should say,
"The Lord will exclude me from his people,"
and the eunuch should not say,
"Look, I am a dried-up tree."
⁴ For the Lord says this:
"For the eunuchs who keep my Sabbaths,
and choose what pleases me,
and hold firmly to my covenant,
⁵ I will give them, in my house and within my walls,
a memorial and a name
better than sons and daughters.
I will give each of them an everlasting name
that will never be cut off.
⁶ As for the foreigners who join themselves to the Lord
to minister to him, to love the name of the Lord,
and to become his servants—
all who keep the Sabbath without desecrating it
and who hold firmly to my covenant—
⁷ I will bring them to my holy mountain
and let them rejoice in my house of prayer.
Their burnt offerings and sacrifices
will be acceptable on my altar,
for my house will be called a house of prayer
for all nations."
⁸ This is the declaration of the Lord God,
who gathers the dispersed of Israel:
"I will gather to them still others
besides those already gathered."

PAUSE HERE

Underline Isaiah 56:7–8,
God's description of who
is welcome to be part of
His people.

MARK 7:24-30

A GENTILE MOTHER'S FAITH

²⁴ He got up and departed from there to the region of Tyre.
He entered a house and did not want anyone to know it,
but he could not escape notice. ²⁵ Instead, immediately after
hearing about him, a woman whose little daughter had an
unclean spirit came and fell at his feet. ²⁶ The woman was a
Gentile, a Syrophoenician by birth, and she was asking him
to cast the demon out of her daughter. ²⁷ He said to her,
"Let the children be fed first, because it isn't right to take the
children's bread and throw it to the dogs."

²⁸ But she replied to him, "Lord, even the dogs under the
table eat the children's crumbs."

²⁹ Then he told her, "Because of this reply, you may go. The
demon has left your daughter." ³⁰ When she went back to her
home, she found her child lying on the bed, and the demon
was gone.

ACTS 8:26-39

THE CONVERSION OF THE
ETHIOPIAN OFFICIAL

²⁶ An angel of the Lord spoke to Philip: "Get up and go
south to the road that goes down from Jerusalem to Gaza."
(This is the desert road.) ²⁷ So he got up and went. There was
an Ethiopian man, a eunuch and high official of Candace,
queen of the Ethiopians, who was in charge of her entire
treasury. He had come to worship in Jerusalem ²⁸ and was
sitting in his chariot on his way home, reading the prophet
Isaiah aloud.

²⁹ The Spirit told Philip, "Go and join that chariot."

³⁰ When Philip ran up to it, he heard him reading the prophet
Isaiah, and said, "Do you understand what you're reading?"

³¹ "How can I," he said, "unless someone guides me?" So
he invited Philip to come up and sit with him. ³² Now the
Scripture passage he was reading was this:

He was led like a sheep to the slaughter,
and as a lamb is silent before its shearer,
so he does not open his mouth.
³³ In his humiliation justice was denied him.
Who will describe his generation?
For his life is taken from the earth.

[34] The eunuch said to Philip, "I ask you, who is the prophet saying this about—himself or someone else?" [35] Philip proceeded to tell him the good news about Jesus, beginning with that Scripture.

[36] As they were traveling down the road, they came to some water. The eunuch said, "Look, there's water. What would keep me from being baptized?" [38] So he ordered the chariot to stop, and both Philip and the eunuch went down into the water, and he baptized him. [39] When they came up out of the water, the Spirit of the Lord carried Philip away, and the eunuch did not see him any longer but went on his way rejoicing.

ROMANS 9:22-26

[22] And what if God, wanting to display his wrath and to make his power known, endured with much patience objects of wrath prepared for destruction?

[23] And what if he did this to make known the riches of his glory on objects of mercy that he prepared beforehand for glory—

[24] on us, the ones he also called, not only from the Jews but also from the Gentiles? [25] As it also says in Hosea,

I will call Not My People, My People,
and she who is Unloved, Beloved.
[26] And it will be in the place where they were told,
you are not my people,
there they will be called sons of the living God.

REVELATION 5:8-13

THE LAMB IS WORTHY

[8] When he took the scroll, the four living creatures and the twenty-four elders fell down before the Lamb. Each one had a harp and golden bowls filled with incense, which are the prayers of the saints. [9] And they sang a new song:

You are worthy to take the scroll
and to open its seals,
because you were slaughtered,
and you purchased people
for God by your blood
from every tribe and language
and people and nation.
[10] You made them a kingdom
and priests to our God,
and they will reign on the earth.

[11] Then I looked and heard the voice of many angels around the throne, and also of the living creatures and of the elders. Their number was countless thousands, plus thousands of thousands. [12] They said with a loud voice,

Worthy is the Lamb who was slaughtered
to receive power and riches
and wisdom and strength
and honor and glory and blessing!

[13] I heard every creature in heaven, on earth, under the earth, on the sea, and everything in them say,

Blessing and honor and glory and power
be to the one seated on the throne,
and to the Lamb, forever and ever!

HOW DOES TODAY'S NEW TESTAMENT
READING REFLECT CHRIST'S FULFILLMENT
OF WHAT YOU READ IN THE OLD TESTAMENT?

Use the space below to respond,
reflect on the reading, journal, or record a prayer.

christmas
& THE SEASONS OF THE CHURCH

• • • • • • • • •

The Advent season is part of the Church calendar, a centuries-old way many Christian denominations order the year to intentionally remember and celebrate the redeeming work of Christ. Structured around the moving date of Easter Sunday and the fixed date of Christmas, the liturgical Church calendar consists of six seasons as well as ordinary time. Here is a brief explanation of the three seasons that are specifically connected to the birth of Jesus: Advent, Christmastide, and Epiphany.

ADVENT

WHAT IS IT?

A season of anticipating the celebration of Jesus's birth, while also anticipating His promised return. The term *advent* comes from a Latin word meaning "coming" or "arrival."

———

WHEN IS IT?

Four Sundays before Christmas Day through December 24.

———

HOW IS IT OBSERVED?

Many Christians mark the four Sundays during Advent by lighting one candle each Sunday and a fifth candle on Christmas Eve. The colors of these candles vary among denominations, but many Protestant traditions use three purple or blue candles (the traditional Church color for Advent), one pink candle, and one white candle. The candles represent the themes of hope, peace, joy, and love.

CHRISTMASTIDE

WHAT IS IT?

A season celebrating the birth of Jesus, also known as the Twelve Days of Christmas and Yuletide.

WHEN IS IT?

December 25 through January 5.

HOW IS IT OBSERVED?

Celebrations in this season revolve around rejoicing in and remembering Jesus's birth; themes of joy, merriment, and goodwill mark Christmastide. Many Christians give gifts, go caroling, attend church services and Christmas nativity plays, and enjoy special meals with each other throughout the twelve-day celebration.

> **KEY SCRIPTURES**
>
> IS 9:2–7; MT 1:18–25;
> LK 1:26–38; 2:1–20

EPIPHANY

WHAT IS IT?

Epiphany comes from a Greek word that means "to manifest" or "to show." It is also known as the Feast of the Three Kings, Three Kings' Day, and Twelfth Night. Epiphany commemorates the arrival of the wise men to Bethlehem and is a reminder that Christ's birth is good news for all creation.

WHEN IS IT?

January 6, twelve days after Christmas. Some traditions celebrate Epiphany as a season through the Sunday before Ash Wednesday, rather than just one day.

HOW IS IT OBSERVED?

While the season is celebrated in different ways across various cultures and religious traditions, it commonly includes singing, church attendance, reciting blessings over homes, gift giving, and eating special food tied to the feast, such as the Three Kings' Cake.

> **KEY SCRIPTURE**
>
> MT 2:1–12

DAY 20

COME, THOU LONG-EXPECTED JESUS,
BORN TO SET THY PEOPLE FREE;
FROM OUR FEARS AND SINS RELEASE US;
LET US FIND OUR REST IN THEE.
ISRAEL'S STRENGTH AND CONSOLATION,
HOPE OF ALL THE EARTH THOU ART;
DEAR DESIRE OF EV'RY NATION,
/   JOY OF EV'RY longing heart.   /

BORN THY PEOPLE TO DELIVER,
BORN A CHILD, AND YET A KING,
BORN TO REIGN IN US FOREVER,
NOW THY GRACIOUS KINGDOM BRING.
BY THINE OWN ETERNAL SPIRIT RULE
IN ALL OUR HEARTS ALONE;
BY THINE ALL-SUFFICIENT MERIT,
RAISE US TO THY GLORIOUS THRONE.

PSALM 16:5-11

5 LORD, you are my portion
and my cup of blessing;
you hold my future.
6 The boundary lines have fallen for me
in pleasant places;
indeed, I have a beautiful inheritance.

7 I will bless the LORD who counsels me—
even at night when my thoughts trouble me.
8 I always let the LORD guide me.
Because he is at my right hand,
I will not be shaken.

9 Therefore my heart is glad
and my whole being rejoices;
my body also rests securely.

10 For you will not abandon me to Sheol;
you will not allow your faithful one to see decay.
11 You reveal the path of life to me;
in your presence is abundant joy;
at your right hand are eternal pleasures.

ISAIAH 55:10-13

10 "For just as rain and snow fall from heaven
and do not return there
without saturating the earth
and making it germinate and sprout,
and providing seed to sow
and food to eat,
11 so my word that comes from my mouth
will not return to me empty,
but it will accomplish what I please
and will prosper in what I send it to do."

12 You will indeed go out with joy
and be peacefully guided;
the mountains and the hills will break into singing
   before you,
and all the trees of the field will clap their hands.

13 Instead of the thornbush, a cypress will come up,
and instead of the brier, a myrtle will come up;
this will stand as a monument for the LORD,
an everlasting sign that will not be destroyed.

PAUSE
———
HERE

Circle any words or images
in the Old Testament
reading that relate to joy.

JOHN 20:1-20

THE EMPTY TOMB

1 On the first day of the week Mary Magdalene came to the tomb early, while it was still dark. She saw that the stone had been removed from the tomb. 2 So she went running to Simon Peter and to the other disciple, the one Jesus loved, and said to them, "They've taken the Lord out of the tomb, and we don't know where they've put him!"

3 At that, Peter and the other disciple went out, heading for the tomb. 4 The two were running together, but the other disciple outran Peter and got to the tomb first. 5 Stooping down, he saw the linen cloths lying there, but he did not go in. 6 Then, following him, Simon Peter also came. He entered the tomb and saw the linen cloths lying there. 7 The wrapping that had been on his head was not lying with the linen cloths but was folded up in a separate place by itself. 8 The other disciple, who had reached the tomb first, then also went in, saw, and believed. 9 For they did not yet understand the Scripture that he must rise from the dead. 10 Then the disciples returned to the place where they were staying.

MARY MAGDALENE SEES THE RISEN LORD

11 But Mary stood outside the tomb, crying. As she was crying, she stooped to look into the tomb. 12 She saw two angels in white sitting where Jesus's body had been lying, one at the head and the other at the feet. 13 They said to her, "Woman, why are you crying?"

"Because they've taken away my Lord," she told them, "and I don't know where they've put him."

¹⁴ Having said this, she turned around and saw Jesus standing there, but she did not know it was Jesus. ¹⁵ "Woman," Jesus said to her, "why are you crying? Who is it that you're seeking?"

Supposing he was the gardener, she replied, "Sir, if you've carried him away, tell me where you've put him, and I will take him away."

¹⁶ Jesus said to her, "Mary."

Turning around, she said to him in Aramaic, *"Rabboni!"*—which means "Teacher."

¹⁷ "Don't cling to me," Jesus told her, "since I have not yet ascended to the Father. But go to my brothers and tell them that I am ascending to my Father and your Father, to my God and your God."

¹⁸ Mary Magdalene went and announced to the disciples, "I have seen the Lord!" And she told them what he had said to her.

THE DISCIPLES COMMISSIONED

¹⁹ When it was evening on that first day of the week, the disciples were gathered together with the doors locked because they feared the Jews. Jesus came, stood among them, and said to them, "Peace be with you."

²⁰ Having said this, he showed them his hands and his side. So the disciples rejoiced when they saw the Lord.

1 PETER 1:3-12

A LIVING HOPE

³ Blessed be the God and Father of our Lord Jesus Christ. Because of his great mercy he has given us new birth into a living hope through the resurrection of Jesus Christ from the dead ⁴ and into an inheritance that is imperishable, undefiled, and unfading, kept in heaven for you. ⁵ You are being guarded by God's power through faith for a salvation that is ready to be revealed in the last time. ⁶ You rejoice in this, even though now for a short time, if necessary, you suffer grief in various trials ⁷ so that the proven character of your faith—more valuable than gold which, though perishable, is refined by fire—may result in praise, glory, and honor at the revelation of Jesus Christ.

⁸ Though you have not seen him, you love him; though not seeing him now, you believe in him, and you rejoice with inexpressible and glorious joy,

⁹ because you are receiving the goal of your faith, the salvation of your souls.

¹⁰ Concerning this salvation, the prophets, who prophesied about the grace that would come to you, searched and carefully investigated. ¹¹ They inquired into what time or what circumstances the Spirit of Christ within them was indicating when he testified in advance to the sufferings of Christ and the glories that would follow. ¹² It was revealed to them that they were not serving themselves but you. These things have now been announced to you through those who preached the gospel to you by the Holy Spirit sent from heaven—angels long to catch a glimpse of these things.

JOHN 16:20-22

²⁰ "Truly I tell you, you will weep and mourn, but the world will rejoice. You will become sorrowful, but your sorrow will turn to joy. ²¹ When a woman is in labor, she has pain because her time has come. But when she has given birth to a child, she no longer remembers the suffering because of the joy that a person has been born into the world. ²² So you also have sorrow now. But I will see you again. Your hearts will rejoice, and no one will take away your joy from you."

WHAT IS IT YOU FIND YOURSELF LONGING FOR THIS HOLIDAY SEASON? HOW DOES TODAY'S NEW TESTAMENT READING CENTER THAT LONGING ON CHRIST?

Use the space below to respond,
reflect on the reading, journal, or record a prayer.

prep time

15 MINUTES / **30–40 MINUTES** / **8**

cook time

serves

ITALIAN SAUSAGE, GNOCCHI & KALE SOUP

1 teaspoon olive oil ☐	In a large dutch oven or stock pot, heat oil over medium heat. Add sausage and brown, breaking apart with a wooden spoon. Add onion and cook until tender (about 5 to 7 minutes), stirring frequently.
1 pound Italian sausage, hot or mild ☐	
1 yellow onion, diced ☐	
Salt and pepper, to taste ☐	Add a pinch of salt and pepper. Add garlic and cook another 2 to 3 minutes. Increase heat to medium-high and add tomatoes, cooking until they begin to soften (about 5 to 10 minutes). Stir frequently. Once tender, reduce heat to medium and gently mash with back of spoon. Let cook for 1 to 2 minutes more.
3 cloves garlic, minced ☐	
16 ounces grape tomatoes, halved ☐	
2 teaspoons Italian seasoning ☐	
7 cups low-sodium chicken broth ☐	Add Italian seasoning, followed by broth to deglaze the pan. Increase heat, cover, and bring to boil. Reduce heat and let simmer 1 to 2 minutes more.
1 pound potato gnocchi ☐	Add gnocchi and cook until they float to the top, about 3 to 5 minutes.
1 cup heavy whipping cream ☐	
3 cups curly kale, chopped ☐	Reduce heat to medium, and add cream and kale. Cook for 1 to 2 minutes until kale is wilted. Take off heat and let soup sit 5 to 10 minutes.
Parmesan cheese, freshly shaved ☐	Add more salt and pepper to taste. Ladle into bowls and top with Parmesan cheese.

Day 21

GRACE DAY

Advent is a season to intentionally
slow our pace, contemplating and
celebrating the first coming of
Christ while also anticipating His
promised return. Take time today
to pause from the busyness of the
season to catch up on your reading,
make space for prayer, and rest in
the presence of the Lord.

Revisit "Advent Rhythms" on pages 18–19 to help reorient
your rhythms of rest and celebration.

THE WORD
became FLESH AND
DWELT among US.
WE OBSERVED HIS
glory, THE GLORY
AS THE one
and ONLY SON
FROM the FATHER,
FULL of GRACE
and TRUTH.

John 1:14

THE FOURTH SUNDAY

of Advent

The angel replied to her, "The Holy
Spirit will come upon you, and the
power of the Most High will overshadow
you. Therefore, the holy one to be born
will be called the Son of God."

Luke 1:35

In 1847, Placide Cappeau was commissioned to write a
Christmas poem. Drawing on the story of Jesus's birth in
the Gospel of Luke, Cappeau composed "O Holy Night."
The night of Christ's birth marked a pivotal stage in salvation
history because the Holy One had come to dwell on earth,
an event that would change every day after it.

O HOLY NIGHT

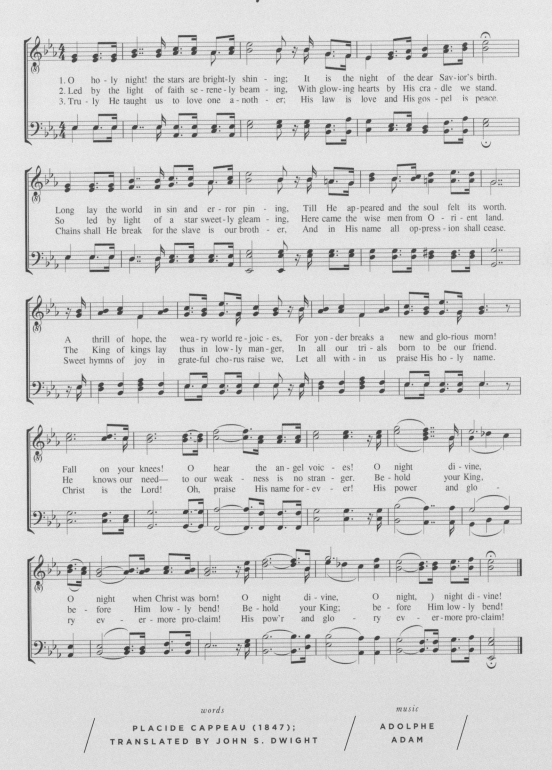

1. O ho - ly night! the stars are bright-ly shin - ing;   It is the night of the dear Sav-ior's birth.
2. Led by the light of faith se - rene-ly beam - ing, With glow-ing hearts by His cra - dle we stand.
3. Tru-ly He taught us to love one a - noth - er;   His law is love and His gos - pel is peace.

Long   lay the world in sin and er - ror pin - ing,   Till He ap-peared and the soul felt its worth.
So   led by light of a star sweet-ly gleam - ing, Here came the wise men from O - ri - ent land.
Chains shall He break for the slave is our broth - er,   And in His name all op-press - ion shall cease.

A   thrill of hope, the   wea-ry world re - joic - es, For yon - der breaks a   new and glo-rious morn!
The   King of kings lay   thus in low-ly man - ger,   In all our tri - als born to be our friend.
Sweet hymns of joy in   grate-ful cho-rus raise we, Let all with - in us   praise His ho - ly name.

Fall   on your knees!   O hear   the an - gel voic - es!   O night   di - vine,
He   knows our need—   to our weak - ness is no stran - ger. Be - hold   your King,
Christ is the Lord!   Oh, praise   His name for - ev - er! His power   and glo -

O   night   when Christ was born!   O night   di - vine,   O   night,) night di - vine!
be - fore Him low - ly bend!   Be - hold   your King;   be - fore   Him low - ly bend!
ry   ev - er - more pro-claim!   His pow'r   and glo - ry   ev - er-more pro-claim!

words

**PLACIDE CAPPEAU (1847);
TRANSLATED BY JOHN S. DWIGHT**

music

**ADOLPHE
ADAM**

DAY 23

COME, THOU LONG-EXPECTED JESUS,
BORN to SET THY PEOPLE free;
FROM our FEARS and SINS RELEASE US;
LET US find our REST IN THEE.
ISRAEL'S STRENGTH and CONSOLATION,
HOPE OF all the earth THOU ART;
DEAR DESIRE OF EV'RY NATION,
JOY OF EV'RY longing heart.

/ BORN THY PEOPLE to deliver, /
BORN A child, AND YET A KING,
BORN TO reign IN US FOREVER,
NOW THY GRACIOUS kingdom BRING.
BY THINE OWN ETERNAL SPIRIT rule
IN ALL OUR HEARTS alone;
BY THINE all-sufficient MERIT,
RAISE US TO THY GLORIOUS throne.

GENESIS 49:10

The scepter will not depart from Judah
or the staff from between his feet
until he whose right it is comes
and the obedience of the peoples belongs to him.

NUMBERS 24:17

I see him, but not now;
I perceive him, but not near.
A star will come from Jacob,
and a scepter will arise from Israel.
He will smash the forehead of Moab
and strike down all the Shethites.

2 SAMUEL 7:8-16

8 "So now this is what you are to say to my servant David:
'This is what the LORD of Armies says: I took you from the
pasture, from tending the flock, to be ruler over my people
Israel. 9 I have been with you wherever you have gone, and
I have destroyed all your enemies before you. I will make a
great name for you like that of the greatest on the earth. 10 I
will designate a place for my people Israel and plant them, so
that they may live there and not be disturbed again. Evildoers
will not continue to oppress them as they have done 11 ever
since the day I ordered judges to be over my people Israel. I
will give you rest from all your enemies.

"'The LORD declares to you: The LORD himself will make a
house for you. 12 When your time comes and you rest with
your ancestors, I will raise up after you your descendant, who
will come from your body, and I will establish his kingdom.
13 He is the one who will build a house for my name, and I
will establish the throne of his kingdom forever. 14 I will be
his father, and he will be my son. When he does wrong, I will
discipline him with a rod of men and blows from mortals.
15 But my faithful love will never leave him as it did when
I removed it from Saul, whom I removed from before you.

16 Your house and kingdom will endure before me forever,
and your throne will be established forever.'"

ISAIAH 7:14

Therefore, the Lord himself will give you a sign: See, the
virgin will conceive, have a son, and name him Immanuel.

ISAIAH 9:2-7

2 The people walking in darkness
have seen a great light;
a light has dawned
on those living in the land of darkness.
3 You have enlarged the nation
and increased its joy.
The people have rejoiced before you
as they rejoice at harvest time
and as they rejoice when dividing spoils.
4 For you have shattered their oppressive yoke
and the rod on their shoulders,
the staff of their oppressor,
just as you did on the day of Midian.
5 For every trampling boot of battle
and the bloodied garments of war
will be burned as fuel for the fire.
6 For a child will be born for us,
a son will be given to us,
and the government will be on his shoulders.
He will be named
Wonderful Counselor, Mighty God,
Eternal Father, Prince of Peace.
7 The dominion will be vast,
and its prosperity will never end.
He will reign on the throne of David
and over his kingdom,
to establish and sustain it
with justice and righteousness from now on and forever.
The zeal of the LORD of Armies will accomplish this.

PAUSE Underline 2 Samuel 7:12 and 7:16, God's promise to King David to raise up an eternal King from his descendants. Circle descriptions in Isaiah 9 of what that King's reign would look like. After this, continue your reading on the next page.

MARK 10:46-52

A BLIND MAN HEALED

[46] They came to Jericho. And as he was leaving Jericho with his disciples and a large crowd, Bartimaeus (the son of Timaeus), a blind beggar, was sitting by the road. [47] When he heard that it was Jesus of Nazareth, he began to cry out,

```
"Jesus, Son of David, have mercy on me!"
```

[48] Many warned him to keep quiet, but he was crying out all the more, "Have mercy on me, Son of David!"

[49] Jesus stopped and said, "Call him."

So they called the blind man and said to him, "Have courage! Get up; he's calling for you." [50] He threw off his coat, jumped up, and came to Jesus.

[51] Then Jesus answered him, "What do you want me to do for you?"

"Rabboni," the blind man said to him, "I want to see."

[52] Jesus said to him, "Go, your faith has saved you." Immediately he could see and began to follow Jesus on the road.

ROMANS 1:1-6

THE GOSPEL OF GOD FOR ROME

[1] Paul, a servant of Christ Jesus, called as an apostle and set apart for the gospel of God— [2] which he promised beforehand through his prophets in the Holy Scriptures— [3] concerning his Son, Jesus Christ our Lord, who was a descendant of David according to the flesh [4] and was appointed to be the powerful Son of God according to the Spirit of holiness by the resurrection of the dead. [5] Through him we have received grace and apostleship to bring about the obedience of faith for the sake of his name among all the Gentiles, [6] including you who are also called by Jesus Christ.

HOW WERE CHRIST'S ACTIONS IN TODAY'S READING A REFLECTION OF THE PROMISED KING'S REIGN? HOW DO YOU SEE THAT SAME ONGOING MINISTRY PRESENT IN YOUR LIFE AND HOW YOU MODEL CHRIST FOR OTHERS?

Use the space below to respond,
reflect on the reading, journal, or record a prayer.

BORN THY PEOPLE
TO DELIVER

DAY 24

2 CHRONICLES 21:7

…but for the sake of the covenant the LORD had made with David, he was unwilling to destroy the house of David since the LORD had promised to give a lamp to David and to his sons forever.

JEREMIAH 33:19-26

[19] The word of the LORD came to Jeremiah: [20] "This is what the LORD says: If you can break my covenant with the day and my covenant with the night so that day and night cease to come at their regular time, [21] then also my covenant with my servant David may be broken. If that could happen, then he would not have a son reigning on his throne and the Levitical priests would not be my ministers. [22] Even as the stars of heaven cannot be counted, and the sand of the sea cannot be measured, so too I will make innumerable the descendants of my servant David and the Levites who minister to me."

[23] The word of the LORD came to Jeremiah: [24] "Have you not noticed what these people have said? They say, 'The LORD has rejected the two families he had chosen.' My people are treated with contempt and no longer regarded as a nation among them. [25] This is what the LORD says: If I do not keep my covenant with the day and with the night, and if I fail to establish the fixed order of heaven and earth, [26] then I might also reject the descendants of Jacob and of my servant David. That is, I would not take rulers from his descendants to rule over the descendants of Abraham, Isaac, and Jacob. But in fact, I will restore their fortunes and have compassion on them."

pause // Circle 2 Chronicles 21:7, God's commitment to keep the promise He made to King David. //

MATTHEW 1:1-17

THE GENEALOGY OF JESUS CHRIST

[1] An account of the genealogy of Jesus Christ, the Son of David, the Son of Abraham:

FROM ABRAHAM TO DAVID

[2] Abraham fathered Isaac,
Isaac fathered Jacob,
Jacob fathered Judah and his brothers,
[3] Judah fathered Perez and Zerah by Tamar,
Perez fathered Hezron,
Hezron fathered Aram,

+

GENEALOGY

Mt 1:1

A curated look at a family line. Jesus's genealogy can be found in both Matthew 1 and Luke 3. Matthew's genealogy was written to a Jewish audience who placed great value on lineage, connecting a person to their family of origin. Matthew's genealogy traces the lineage from Abraham to Mary, while Luke's genealogy traces the lineage back from Joseph to Adam.

⁴ Aram fathered Amminadab,
Amminadab fathered Nahshon,
Nahshon fathered Salmon,
⁵ Salmon fathered Boaz by Rahab,
Boaz fathered Obed by Ruth,
Obed fathered Jesse,
⁶ and Jesse fathered King David.

FROM DAVID TO THE
BABYLONIAN EXILE

David fathered Solomon by Uriah's wife,
⁷ Solomon fathered Rehoboam,
Rehoboam fathered Abijah,
Abijah fathered Asa,
⁸ Asa fathered Jehoshaphat,
Jehoshaphat fathered Joram,
Joram fathered Uzziah,
⁹ Uzziah fathered Jotham,
Jotham fathered Ahaz,
Ahaz fathered Hezekiah,
¹⁰ Hezekiah fathered Manasseh,
Manasseh fathered Amon,
Amon fathered Josiah,
¹¹ and Josiah fathered Jeconiah and
his brothers
at the time of the exile to Babylon.

FROM THE EXILE TO THE MESSIAH

¹² After the exile to Babylon
Jeconiah fathered Shealtiel,
Shealtiel fathered Zerubbabel,
¹³ Zerubbabel fathered Abiud,
Abiud fathered Eliakim,
Eliakim fathered Azor,
¹⁴ Azor fathered Zadok,
Zadok fathered Achim,
Achim fathered Eliud,
¹⁵ Eliud fathered Eleazar,
Eleazar fathered Matthan,
Matthan fathered Jacob,

¹⁶ and Jacob fathered Joseph the husband
of Mary,
who gave birth to Jesus who is called
the Messiah.

¹⁷ So all the generations from Abraham to
David were fourteen generations; and from
David until the exile to Babylon, fourteen
generations; and from the exile to Babylon
until the Messiah, fourteen generations.

REVELATION 19:11-16

THE RIDER ON A WHITE HORSE

¹¹ Then I saw heaven opened, and there was
a white horse. Its rider is called Faithful and
True, and with justice he judges and makes
war. ¹² His eyes were like a fiery flame, and
many crowns were on his head. He had a name
written that no one knows except himself.
¹³ He wore a robe dipped in blood, and
his name is called the Word of God. ¹⁴ The
armies that were in heaven followed him on
white horses, wearing pure white linen. ¹⁵ A
sharp sword came from his mouth, so that he
might strike the nations with it. He will rule
them with an iron rod. He will also trample
the winepress of the fierce anger of God, the
Almighty. ¹⁶ And he has a name written on his
robe and on his thigh: KING OF KINGS AND
LORD OF LORDS.

REVELATION 22:16

"I, Jesus, have sent my angel to attest these
things to you for the churches.

I am the Root and descendant
of David,

the bright morning star."

MESSIAH

Mt 1:16

The Hebrew word
mashiach, or
"messiah," used to
refer to the promised
Savior of God's
people. The word was
translated into the
Greek as *christos*,
which is translated
into English as
"Christ." "Messiah"
and "Christ" are
two titles that
describe Jesus as the
Anointed, or chosen,
One of Israel. In
the Old Testament,
prophets, priests,
and kings were
anointed with oil
to ceremonially set
them apart for their
particular work. In
the book of Matthew,
this title is used to
affirm Jesus as the
chosen and Anointed
One who perfectly
fulfilled His calling
as the Savior of
God's people.

**WHERE IN TODAY'S NEW TESTAMENT READING
DO YOU SEE GOD'S COMMITMENT TO FULFILL
HIS PROMISE TO KING DAVID IN CHRIST?**

————————

Use the space below to respond,
reflect on the reading, journal, or record a prayer.

BORN THY PEOPLE TO DELIVER

ISAIAH 40:3-5

³ A voice of one crying out:

Prepare the way of the LORD in the wilderness;
make a straight highway for our God in the desert.
⁴ Every valley will be lifted up,
and every mountain and hill will be leveled;
the uneven ground will become smooth
and the rough places, a plain.
⁵ And the glory of the LORD will appear,
and all humanity together will see it,
for the mouth of the LORD has spoken.

 Underline Isaiah 40:3 and 40:5,
God's promise of the one who would
prepare the way for the Messiah.

LUKE 1:57-80

THE BIRTH AND NAMING OF JOHN

⁵⁷ Now the time had come for Elizabeth to give birth, and she had a son. ⁵⁸ Then her neighbors and relatives heard that the Lord had shown her his great mercy, and they rejoiced with her.

⁵⁹ When they came to circumcise the child on the eighth day, they were going to name him Zechariah, after his father. ⁶⁰ But his mother responded, "No. He will be called John."

⁶¹ Then they said to her, "None of your relatives has that name." ⁶² So they motioned to his father to find out what he wanted him to be called. ⁶³ He asked for a writing tablet and wrote, "His name is John." And they were all amazed. ⁶⁴ Immediately his mouth was opened and his tongue set free, and he began to speak, praising God. ⁶⁵ Fear came on all those who lived around them, and all these things were being talked about throughout the hill country of Judea. ⁶⁶ All who heard about him took it to heart, saying, "What then will this child become?" For, indeed, the Lord's hand was with him.

ZECHARIAH'S PROPHECY

⁶⁷ Then his father Zechariah was filled with the Holy Spirit and prophesied:

⁶⁸ Blessed is the Lord, the God of Israel,
because he has visited
and provided redemption for his people.

69 He has raised up a horn of salvation for us
in the house of his servant David,
70 just as he spoke by the mouth
of his holy prophets in ancient times;
71 salvation from our enemies
and from the hand of those who hate us.
72 He has dealt mercifully with our ancestors
and remembered his holy covenant—
73 the oath that he swore to our
    father Abraham,
to grant that we,
74 having been rescued
from the hand of our enemies,
would serve him without fear
75 in holiness and righteousness
in his presence all our days.
76 And you, child, will be called
a prophet of the Most High,
for you will go before the Lord
to prepare his ways,
77 to give his people knowledge of salvation
through the forgiveness of their sins.
78 Because of our God's merciful compassion,
the dawn from on high will visit us
79 to shine on those who live in darkness
and the shadow of death,
to guide our feet into the way of peace.

80 The child grew up and became strong in spirit,
and he was in the wilderness until the day of his
public appearance to Israel.

JOHN 1:6–9, 15

6 There was a man sent from God whose name
was John. 7 He came as a witness to testify about
the light, so that all might believe through him.
8 He was not the light, but he came to testify
about the light. 9 The true light that gives light to
everyone was coming into the world.

…

✝ MOST HIGH

Lk 1:76

Indicates God's
place, rank, and
power above all
else. There is
none higher, or of
greater authority,
than God.

---

15 (John testified concerning him and exclaimed,
"This was the one of whom I said, 'The one
coming after me ranks ahead of me, because he
existed before me.'")

MATTHEW 11:1–10

JOHN THE BAPTIST DOUBTS

1 When Jesus had finished giving instructions
to his twelve disciples, he moved on from there
to teach and preach in their towns. 2 Now when
John heard in prison what the Christ was doing,
he sent a message through his disciples 3 and
asked him, "Are you the one who is to come, or
should we expect someone else?"

4 Jesus replied to them, "Go and report to John
what you hear and see: 5 The blind receive their
sight, the lame walk, those with leprosy are
cleansed, the deaf hear, the dead are raised, and
the poor are told the good news, 6 and blessed is
the one who isn't offended by me."

7 As these men were leaving, Jesus began to
speak to the crowds about John: "What did
you go out into the wilderness to see? A reed
swaying in the wind? 8 What then did you go
out to see? A man dressed in soft clothes? See,
those who wear soft clothes are in royal palaces.
9 What then did you go out to see? A prophet?
Yes, I tell you, and more than a prophet. 10 This
is the one about whom it is written:

See, I am sending my messenger ahead of you;
he will prepare your way before you."

HOW DOES ZECHARIAH'S SONG REFLECT THE PROPHECY GIVEN IN ISAIAH? AS JOHN THE BAPTIST PREPARED A WAY FOR THE COMING MESSIAH, HOW CAN WE PREPARE OUR OWN HEARTS TO CELEBRATE CHRIST'S COMING TO US?

———————

Use the space below to respond,
reflect on the reading, journal, or record a prayer.

BORN THY PEOPLE
TO DELIVER

DAY 26

PSALM 107:1-6

THANKSGIVING FOR GOD'S DELIVERANCE

[1] Give thanks to the LORD, for he is good;
his faithful love endures forever.
[2] Let the redeemed of the LORD proclaim
that he has redeemed them from the power of the foe
[3] and has gathered them from the lands—
from the east and the west,
from the north and the south.

[4] Some wandered in the desolate wilderness,
finding no way to a city where they could live.
[5] They were hungry and thirsty;
their spirits failed within them.
[6] Then they cried out to the LORD in their trouble;
he rescued them from their distress.

PAUSE
—
HERE

Underline Psalm 107:2 and 107:6,
anticipation that God would
deliver His people.

LUKE 1:26-56

GABRIEL PREDICTS JESUS'S BIRTH

[26] In the sixth month, the angel Gabriel was sent by God to a town in Galilee called Nazareth, [27] to a virgin engaged to a man named Joseph, of the house of David. The virgin's name was Mary. [28] And the angel came to her and said, "Greetings, favored woman! The Lord is with you." [29] But she was deeply troubled by this statement, wondering what kind of greeting this could be. [30] Then the angel told her, "Do not be afraid, Mary, for you have found favor with God. [31] Now listen: You will conceive and give birth to a son, and you will name him Jesus. [32] He will be great and will be called the Son of the Most High, and the Lord God will give him the throne of his father David. [33] He will reign over the house of Jacob forever, and his kingdom will have no end."

[34] Mary asked the angel, "How can this be, since I have not had sexual relations with a man?"

[35] The angel replied to her, "The Holy Spirit will come upon you, and the power of the Most High will overshadow you. Therefore, the holy one to be born will be called the Son of God. [36] And consider your relative Elizabeth—even she has conceived a son in her old age, and this is the sixth month for her who was called childless. [37] For nothing will be impossible with God."

GABRIEL

Lk 1:28

One of only two named
angels in the Bible.
Gabriel was significant
in the book of Daniel,
where he interprets
Daniel's vision and
discloses prophecy
concerning Judah's
future (Dn 8–10). In the
New Testament, Gabriel
announces the births of
both John the Baptist
and Jesus.

³⁸ "See, I am the Lord's servant," said Mary. "May it happen to me as you have said." Then the angel left her.

MARY'S VISIT TO ELIZABETH

³⁹ In those days Mary set out and hurried to a town in the hill country of Judah ⁴⁰ where she entered Zechariah's house and greeted Elizabeth. ⁴¹ When Elizabeth heard Mary's greeting, the baby leaped inside her, and Elizabeth was filled with the Holy Spirit. ⁴² Then she exclaimed with a loud cry, "Blessed are you among women, and your child will be blessed! ⁴³ How could this happen to me, that the mother of my Lord should come to me? ⁴⁴ For you see, when the sound of your greeting reached my ears, the baby leaped for joy inside me. ⁴⁵ Blessed is she who has believed that the Lord would fulfill what he has spoken to her!"

MARY'S PRAISE

⁴⁶ And Mary said:

> My soul magnifies the Lord,
> ⁴⁷ and my spirit rejoices in God my Savior,
> ⁴⁸ because he has looked with favor
> on the humble condition of his servant.
> Surely, from now on all generations
> will call me blessed,
> ⁴⁹ because the Mighty One
> has done great things for me,
> and his name is holy.
> ⁵⁰ His mercy is from generation to generation
> on those who fear him.
> ⁵¹ He has done a mighty deed with his arm;
> he has scattered the proud
> because of the thoughts of their hearts;
> ⁵² he has toppled the mighty from their thrones
> and exalted the lowly.
> ⁵³ He has satisfied the hungry with good things
> and sent the rich away empty.
> ⁵⁴ He has helped his servant Israel,
> remembering his mercy
> ⁵⁵ to Abraham and his descendants forever,
> just as he spoke to our ancestors.

⁵⁶ And Mary stayed with her about three months; then she returned to her home.

HOW DOES MARY'S RESPONSE OF OBEDIENCE AND PRAISE MODEL FOR US THE HOPE OF DELIVERANCE THAT WE CELEBRATE DURING ADVENT?

———————

Use the space below to respond,
reflect on the reading, journal, or record a prayer.

Born Thy People

/ TO DELIVER /

Day 27

1 SAMUEL 16:1–13

SAMUEL ANOINTS DAVID

¹ The Lᴏʀᴅ said to Samuel, "How long are you going to mourn for Saul, since I have rejected him as king over Israel? Fill your horn with oil and go. I am sending you to Jesse of Bethlehem because I have selected for myself a king from his sons."

² Samuel asked, "How can I go? Saul will hear about it and kill me!"

The Lᴏʀᴅ answered, "Take a young cow with you and say, 'I have come to sacrifice to the Lᴏʀᴅ.' ³ Then invite Jesse to the sacrifice, and I will let you know what you are to do. You are to anoint for me the one I indicate to you."

⁴ Samuel did what the Lᴏʀᴅ directed and went to Bethlehem. When the elders of the town met him, they trembled and asked, "Do you come in peace?"

⁵ "In peace," he replied. "I've come to sacrifice to the Lᴏʀᴅ. Consecrate yourselves and come with me to the sacrifice." Then he consecrated Jesse and his sons and invited them to the sacrifice. ⁶ When they arrived, Samuel saw Eliab and said, "Certainly the Lᴏʀᴅ's anointed one is here before him."

⁷ But the Lᴏʀᴅ said to Samuel, "Do not look at his appearance or his stature because I have rejected him. Humans do not see what the Lᴏʀᴅ sees, for humans see what is visible, but the Lᴏʀᴅ sees the heart."

⁸ Jesse called Abinadab and presented him to Samuel. "The Lᴏʀᴅ hasn't chosen this one either," Samuel said. ⁹ Then Jesse presented Shammah, but Samuel said, "The Lᴏʀᴅ hasn't chosen this one either." ¹⁰ After Jesse presented seven of his sons to him, Samuel told Jesse, "The Lᴏʀᴅ hasn't chosen any of these." ¹¹ Samuel asked him, "Are these all the sons you have?"

"There is still the youngest," he answered, "but right now he's tending the sheep." Samuel told Jesse, "Send for him. We won't sit down to eat until he gets here." ¹² So Jesse sent for him. He had beautiful eyes and a healthy, handsome appearance.

Then the Lᴏʀᴅ said, "Anoint him, for he is the one." ¹³ So Samuel took the horn of oil and anointed him in the presence of his brothers, and the

/ TAKE NOTE /

Spirit of the LORD came powerfully on David from that day forward. Then Samuel set out and went to Ramah.

pause // Underline 1 Samuel 16:7, God's description of what He sees when He looks at His people. //

MATTHEW 1:18-25

THE NATIVITY OF THE MESSIAH

[18] The birth of Jesus Christ came about this way: After his mother Mary had been engaged to Joseph, it was discovered before they came together that she was pregnant from the Holy Spirit. [19] So her husband, Joseph, being a righteous man, and not wanting to disgrace her publicly, decided to divorce her secretly.

[20] But after he had considered these things, an angel of the Lord appeared to him in a dream, saying, "Joseph, son of David, don't be afraid to take Mary as your wife, because what has been conceived in her is from the Holy Spirit. [21] She will give birth to a son, and you are to name him Jesus, because he will save his people from their sins."

[22] Now all this took place to fulfill what was spoken by the Lord through the prophet:

[23] See, the virgin will become pregnant
and give birth to a son,
and they will name him Immanuel,

which is translated "God is with us."

[24] When Joseph woke up, he did as the Lord's angel had commanded him. He married her [25] but did not have sexual relations with her until she gave birth to a son. And he named him Jesus.

1 CORINTHIANS 1:26-31

BOASTING ONLY IN THE LORD

[26] Brothers and sisters, consider your calling: Not many were wise from a human perspective, not many powerful, not many of noble birth. [27] Instead, God has chosen what is foolish in the world to shame the wise, and God has chosen what is weak in the world to shame the strong. [28] God has chosen what is insignificant and despised in the world—what is viewed as nothing—to bring to nothing what is viewed as something, [29] so that no one may boast in his presence. [30] It is from him that you are in Christ Jesus, who became wisdom from God for us—our righteousness, sanctification, and redemption— [31] in order that, as it is written: Let the one who boasts, boast in the Lord.

ENGAGED

Mt 1:18

A first century legal status that could only be broken by death or divorce (also known as a "betrothal"). After a period of typically one year, a marriage ceremony took place, and the woman would move into the man's house. Consummation of the marriage took place after these events.

HOW DOES TODAY'S NEW TESTAMENT READING DEMONSTRATE GOD WORKING IN AN UNEXPECTED WAY? HOW DOES THE ADVENT SEASON REFLECT THIS REALITY?

———

Use the space below to respond,
reflect on the reading, journal, or record a prayer.

CHOCOLATE
pretzel rods

total time

40 MINUTES

yields

30-35 PRETZEL RODS

- ☐ *1 TO 2 POUNDS WHITE OR MILK BAKING CHOCOLATE*
- ☐ *ASSORTED TOPPINGS (SPRINKLES, MINI CHOCOLATE-COATED CANDY PIECES, CRUSHED PEPPERMINT, CRUSHED NUTS, SHREDDED COCONUT, MINI CHOCOLATE CHIPS, ETC.)*
- ☐ *OIL-BASED FOOD COLORING (IF USING WHITE CHOCOLATE)*
- ☐ *1 LARGE BAG 6-TO-8-INCH PRETZEL RODS*
- ☐ *PIPING BAG*

INSTRUCTIONS

Line a cookie sheet with parchment paper.

Place 1 pound of desired chocolate in a microwave-safe bowl. Heat for 30 seconds, then remove and stir. Continue heating for 30-second intervals, stirring between, until chocolate has completely melted. Chocolate should have a ribbon-like consistency. Do not overheat.

If you are using white chocolate and want to add any color, add food coloring once it's melted and stir until desired shade is reached.

OPTIONS

DIPPED RODS

Pour chocolate into a tall vessel, such as a clear drinking glass. Tilt the glass to allow for a larger dipping surface. Insert the pretzel rod, twisting to achieve an even coat.

Place dipped rod onto parchment and immediately garnish with desired toppings.

DRIZZLED RODS

Place melted chocolate into a piping bag and snip off ⅓ of an inch from one corner. Drizzle chocolate over pretzel rods and then place on parchment paper.

If the chocolate inside your piping bag begins to harden, reheat in the microwave in 10-second intervals.

Allow rods to cool before handling. Store in an airtight container for up to 3 weeks.

SHE READS TRUTH
141

CHRISTMAS eve!

WHEN THE TIME CAME TO COMPLETION, GOD SENT HIS SON.

Galatians 4:4

DAY 28

COME, THOU LONG-EXPECTED JESUS,
BORN TO SET THY PEOPLE FREE;
FROM OUR FEARS AND SINS RELEASE US;
LET US FIND OUR REST IN THEE.
ISRAEL'S STRENGTH AND CONSOLATION,
HOPE OF ALL THE EARTH THOU ART;
DEAR DESIRE OF EV'RY NATION,
JOY OF EV'RY LONGING HEART.

BORN THY PEOPLE TO DELIVER,
/ BORN A CHILD, AND YET A KING, /
BORN TO REIGN IN US FOREVER,
NOW THY GRACIOUS KINGDOM BRING.
BY THINE OWN ETERNAL SPIRIT RULE
IN ALL OUR HEARTS ALONE;
BY THINE ALL-SUFFICIENT MERIT,
RAISE US TO THY GLORIOUS THRONE.

MICAH 5:2-5

[2] Bethlehem Ephrathah,
you are small among the clans of Judah;

one will come from you
to be ruler over Israel for me.

His origin is from antiquity,
from ancient times.
[3] Therefore, Israel will be abandoned until the time
when she who is in labor has given birth;
then the rest of the ruler's brothers will return
to the people of Israel.
[4] He will stand and shepherd them
in the strength of the LORD,
in the majestic name of the LORD his God.
They will live securely,
for then his greatness will extend
to the ends of the earth.
[5] He will be their peace.
When Assyria invades our land,
when it marches against our fortresses,
we will raise against it seven shepherds,
even eight leaders of men.

> **PAUSE HERE**
> In today's Old Testament reading, circle the promises about the one who would come to rule over Israel.

LUKE 2:1-20

THE BIRTH OF JESUS

[1] In those days a decree went out from Caesar Augustus that the whole empire should be registered. [2] This first registration took place while Quirinius was governing Syria. [3] So everyone went to be registered, each to his own town.

[4] Joseph also went up from the town of Nazareth in Galilee, to Judea, to the city of David, which is called Bethlehem, because he was of the house and family line of David, [5] to be registered along with Mary, who was engaged to him and was pregnant. [6] While they were there, the time came for her to give

DECREE

Lk 2:1

A public declaration or ordinance issued by a ruler or governing body that carried legal power. Decrees were often delivered in person, spoken aloud, then followed with a written statement.

REGISTRATION

Lk 2:2

Sometimes translated as "census" or "enrollment." An official count of the existing population performed by the government. A registration often took place for the purpose of taxation or preparation for war.

CITY OF DAVID, OR BETHLEHEM

Lk 2:4

A city about five miles southwest of Jerusalem whose name means "house of bread." Bethlehem is the city where David was anointed to be king (1Sm 16:1–13) and is also believed to have been his home (1Sm 17:12, 15).

+

MANGER

`Lk 2:7`

A word meaning "feeding trough" or "stable." This feeding trough for animals could have been located in a cave or a stable, which often was attached to or existed on the lower level of a house. Though the Gospel accounts don't mention any animals, many people believe that the mention of a manger means animals were present when Jesus was born.

MULTITUDE OF THE HEAVENLY HOST

`Lk 2:13`

The Hebrew word *tsava*, or "hosts," used more than 400 times in the Old Testament. *Tsava* refers to both human and angelic armies, as well as stars and planets. One of God's names throughout Scripture is the Lord of Hosts, indicating His rule over His angelic army, as well as the heavens and earth. The New Testament use of "host" also refers to armies of angels. The shepherds encountered what may have seemed to be paradoxical—an army declaring peace (Lk 2:13–14).

birth. [7] Then she gave birth to her firstborn son, and she wrapped him tightly in cloth and laid him in a manger, because there was no guest room available for them.

THE SHEPHERDS AND THE ANGELS

[8] In the same region, shepherds were staying out in the fields and keeping watch at night over their flock. [9] Then an angel of the Lord stood before them, and the glory of the Lord shone around them, and they were terrified. [10] But the angel said to them, "Don't be afraid, for look, I proclaim to you good news of great joy that will be for all the people:

[11] Today in the city of David a Savior was born for you, who is the Messiah, the Lord.

[12] This will be the sign for you: You will find a baby wrapped tightly in cloth and lying in a manger."

[13] Suddenly there was a multitude of the heavenly host with the angel, praising God and saying:

[14] Glory to God in the highest heaven,
and peace on earth to people he favors!

[15] When the angels had left them and returned to heaven, the shepherds said to one another, "Let's go straight to Bethlehem and see what has happened, which the Lord has made known to us."

[16] They hurried off and found both Mary and Joseph, and the baby who was lying in the manger. [17] After seeing them, they reported the message they were told about this child, [18] and all who heard it were amazed at what the shepherds said to them. [19] But Mary was treasuring up all these things in her heart and meditating on them. [20] The shepherds returned, glorifying and praising God for all the things they had seen and heard, which were just as they had been told.

GALATIANS 4:4-5

[4] When the time came to completion, God sent his Son, born of a woman, born under the law, [5] to redeem those under the law, so that we might receive adoption as sons.

HOW IS THE ANTICIPATION OF THE ADVENT SEASON SATISFIED IN TODAY'S NEW TESTAMENT READING?

Use the space below to respond,
reflect on the reading, journal, or record a prayer.

CHRISTMAS day!

BORN A CHILD, AND YET A KING

DAY 29

ISAIAH 2:2-3

2 In the last days
the mountain of the Lord's house will be established
at the top of the mountains
and will be raised above the hills.
All nations will stream to it,
3 and many peoples will come and say,
"Come, let's go up to the mountain of the Lord,
to the house of the God of Jacob.
He will teach us about his ways
so that we may walk in his paths."
For instruction will go out of Zion
and the word of the Lord from Jerusalem.

JEREMIAH 31:15-17

LAMENT TURNED TO JOY

15 This is what the Lord says:

A voice was heard in Ramah,
a lament with bitter weeping—
Rachel weeping for her children,
refusing to be comforted for her children
because they are no more.

16 This is what the Lord says:

Keep your voice from weeping
and your eyes from tears,
for the reward for your work will come—
this is the Lord's declaration—
and your children will return from the enemy's land.

17 There is hope for your future—
this is the Lord's declaration—
and your children will return to their own territory.

 PAUSE Underline parts of the Old Testament reading that point to Israel's future hope.

MATTHEW 2

WISE MEN VISIT THE KING

1 After Jesus was born in Bethlehem of Judea in the days of King Herod, wise men from the east arrived in Jerusalem, 2 saying, "Where is he who has been born king of the Jews? For we saw his star at its rising and have come to worship him."

3 When King Herod heard this, he was deeply disturbed, and all Jerusalem with him. 4 So he assembled all the chief priests and scribes of the people and asked them where the Messiah would be born.

5 "In Bethlehem of Judea," they told him, "because this is what was written by the prophet:

6 And you, Bethlehem, in the land of Judah,
are by no means least among the rulers of Judah:
Because out of you will come a ruler
who will shepherd my people Israel."

7 Then Herod secretly summoned the wise men and asked them the exact time the star appeared. 8 He sent them to

Bethlehem and said, "Go and search carefully for the child. When you find him, report back to me so that I too can go and worship him."

9 After hearing the king, they went on their way. And there it was— the star they had seen at its rising. It led them until it came and stopped above the place where the child was. 10 When they saw the star, they were overwhelmed with joy. 11 Entering the house, they saw the child with Mary his mother, and falling to their knees, they worshiped him. Then they opened their treasures and presented him with gifts: gold, frankincense, and myrrh. 12 And being warned in a dream not to go back to Herod, they returned to their own country by another route.

THE FLIGHT INTO EGYPT

13 After they were gone, an angel of the Lord appeared to Joseph in a dream, saying, "Get up! Take the child and his mother, flee to Egypt, and stay there until I tell you. For Herod is about to search for the child to kill him." 14 So he got up, took the child and his mother during the night, and escaped to Egypt. 15 He stayed there until Herod's death, so that what was spoken by the Lord through the prophet might be fulfilled: Out of Egypt I called my Son.

THE MASSACRE OF THE INNOCENTS

16 Then Herod, when he realized that he had been outwitted by the wise men, flew into a rage. He gave orders to massacre all the boys in and around Bethlehem who were two years old and under, in keeping with the time he had learned from the wise men.

17 Then what was spoken through Jeremiah the prophet was fulfilled:

18 A voice was heard in Ramah,

weeping, and great mourning,
Rachel weeping for her children;
and she refused to be consoled,
because they are no more.

THE RETURN TO NAZARETH

19 After Herod died, an angel of the Lord appeared in a dream to Joseph in Egypt, 20 saying, "Get up, take the child and his mother, and go to the land of Israel, because those who intended to kill the child are dead." 21 So he got up, took the child and his mother, and entered the land of Israel. 22 But when he heard that Archelaus was ruling over Judea in place of his father Herod, he was afraid to go there. And being warned in a dream, he withdrew to the region of Galilee. 23 Then he went and settled in a town called Nazareth to fulfill what was spoken through the prophets, that he would be called a Nazarene.

HEBREWS 1:1-3

THE NATURE OF THE SON

1 Long ago God spoke to our ancestors by the prophets at different times and in different ways. 2 In these last days, he has spoken to us by his Son. God has appointed him heir of all things and made the universe through him. 3 The Son is the radiance of God's glory and the exact expression of his nature, sustaining all things by his powerful word. After making purification for sins, he sat down at the right hand of the Majesty on high.

+

GOLD, FRANKINCENSE, AND MYRRH

Mt 2:11

Gifts that may have funded Joseph, Mary, and Jesus's flight to Egypt. Gold, a costly metal, was typically reserved for items of great significance. Frankincense, an expensive extract from plants, was used in making sacrifices in the tabernacle. Myrrh, another expensive extract from plants, was often used for perfumes and anointing oil in various worship practices. Many scholars believe that this gift foreshadowed Jesus's own sacrificial death on the cross because of two later instances of myrrh in Jesus's life (Mk 15:23; Jn 19:39).

RAMAH

Mt 2:18

A city in ancient Israel. This quote, from the book of Jeremiah, originally described the grief of mothers in Israel as they mourned their sons being carried away into exile. The captives were gathered in Ramah and then taken to Babylon. Here in Matthew, the quote is used to describe another situation in which the mothers of Israel grieve the loss of their sons.

RACHEL

Mt 2:18

A key figure in the Old Testament as the daughter of Laban, wife of Jacob, and mother to Joseph and Benjamin. She died during Benjamin's birth and was buried near Ramah. In Jeremiah's prophecy, Rachel represents all the mothers in Israel, crying not only for her actual descendants (the Benjamites) but for all the captives.

ON THIS CHRISTMAS DAY, HOW DOES THE NEW TESTAMENT READING DEMONSTRATE HOPE FULFILLED IN JESUS BEYOND ANY EARTHLY LONGING?

Use the space below to respond,
reflect on the reading, journal, or record a prayer.

CHRISTMAS DAY SNAPSHOT

WHERE DID I SPEND CHRISTMAS DAY?

WHAT TIME DID I WAKE UP?

AM
___
PM

WHAT WAS THE WEATHER LIKE?

(circle one)

O

HIGH

O

LOW

Who did I celebrate with?

_____

_____

_____

_____

_____

WHAT MADE ME LAUGH?

WHAT TRADITION MEANT
THE MOST TO ME THIS YEAR?

I LOVED GIVING

GIFT

TO

I LOVED RECEIVING

GIFT

FROM

Day 30

born to
reign in us
forever

GENESIS 14:17-20

MELCHIZEDEK'S BLESSING

¹⁷ After Abram returned from defeating Chedorlaomer and the kings who were with him, the king of Sodom went out to meet him in the Shaveh Valley (that is, the King's Valley). ¹⁸ Melchizedek, king of Salem, brought out bread and wine; he was a priest to God Most High. ¹⁹ He blessed him and said:

Abram is blessed by God Most High,
Creator of heaven and earth,
²⁰ and blessed be God Most High
who has handed over your enemies to you.

And Abram gave him a tenth of everything.

PSALM 110:1-4

THE PRIESTLY KING

A psalm of David.

¹ This is the declaration of the LORD
to my Lord:
"Sit at my right hand
until I make your enemies your footstool."
² The LORD will extend your mighty scepter from Zion.
Rule over your surrounding enemies.
³ Your people will volunteer
on your day of battle.
In holy splendor, from the womb of the dawn,
the dew of your youth belongs to you.
⁴ The LORD has sworn an oath and will not take it back:
"You are a priest forever
according to the pattern of Melchizedek."

PAUSE

HERE

Draw a box around every occurrence of the word "king" in your Old Testament reading, and a circle around every occurrence of the word "priest."

MATTHEW 21:1-9

THE TRIUMPHAL ENTRY

¹ When they approached Jerusalem and came to Bethphage at the Mount of Olives, Jesus then sent two disciples, ² telling them, "Go into the village ahead of you. At once you will find a donkey tied there with her colt. Untie them and bring them to me. ³ If anyone says anything to you, say that the Lord needs them, and he will send them at once."

⁴ This took place so that what was spoken through the prophet might be fulfilled:

⁵ Tell Daughter Zion,
"See, your King is coming to you,
gentle, and mounted on a donkey,
and on a colt,
the foal of a donkey."

⁶ The disciples went and did just as Jesus directed them. ⁷ They brought the donkey and the colt; then they laid their clothes on them, and he sat on them. ⁸ A very large crowd spread their clothes on the road; others were cutting branches from the trees and spreading them on the road. ⁹ Then the crowds who went ahead of him and those who followed shouted:

Hosanna to the Son of David!
Blessed is he who comes in the name
of the Lord!
Hosanna in the highest heaven!

HEBREWS 7:1-3, 11-28

THE GREATNESS OF MELCHIZEDEK

¹ For this Melchizedek, king of Salem, priest of God Most High, met Abraham and blessed him as he returned from defeating the kings, ² and Abraham gave him a tenth of everything. First, his name means king of righteousness,

then also, king of Salem, meaning king of peace. ³ Without father, mother, or genealogy, having neither beginning of days nor end of life, but resembling the Son of God, he remains a priest forever.

…

¹¹ Now if perfection came through the Levitical priesthood (for on the basis of it the people received the law), what further need was there for another priest to appear, said to be according to the order of Melchizedek and not according to the order of Aaron? ¹² For when there is a change of the priesthood, there must be a change of law as well. ¹³ For the one these things are spoken about belonged to a different tribe. No one from it has served at the altar. ¹⁴ Now it is evident that our Lord came from Judah, and Moses said nothing about that tribe concerning priests.

¹⁵ And this becomes clearer if another priest like Melchizedek appears, ¹⁶ who did not become a priest based on a legal regulation about physical descent but based on the power of an indestructible life. ¹⁷ For it has been testified:

> You are a priest forever
> according to the order of Melchizedek.

¹⁸ So the previous command is annulled because it was weak and unprofitable ¹⁹ (for the law perfected nothing), but a better hope is introduced, through which we draw near to God.

²⁰ None of this happened without an oath. For others became priests without an oath, ²¹ but he became a priest with an oath made by the one who said to him:

> The Lord has sworn
> and will not change his mind,
> "You are a priest forever."

²² Because of this oath, Jesus has also become the guarantee of a better covenant.

²³ Now many have become Levitical priests, since they are prevented by death from remaining in office. ²⁴ But because he remains forever, he holds his priesthood permanently. ²⁵ Therefore, he is able to save completely those who come to God through him, since he always lives to intercede for them.

²⁶ For this is the kind of high priest we need: holy, innocent, undefiled, separated from sinners, and exalted above the heavens. ²⁷ He doesn't need to offer sacrifices every day, as high priests do—first for their own sins, then for those of the people. He did this once for all time when he offered himself. ²⁸ For the law appoints as high priests men who are weak, but the promise of the oath, which came after the law, appoints a Son, who has been perfected forever.

ROMANS 10:4-13

⁴ For Christ is the end of the law for righteousness to everyone who believes, ⁵ since Moses writes about the righteousness that is from the law: The one who does these things will live by them. ⁶ But the righteousness that comes from faith speaks like this: Do not say in your heart, "Who will go up to heaven?" that is, to bring Christ down ⁷ or, "Who will go down into the abyss?" that is, to bring Christ up from the dead. ⁸ On the contrary, what does it say? The message is near you, in your mouth and in your heart. This is the message of faith that we proclaim: ⁹ If you confess with your mouth, "Jesus is Lord," and believe in your heart that God raised him from the dead, you will be saved. ¹⁰ One believes with the heart, resulting in righteousness, and one confesses with the mouth, resulting in salvation. ¹¹ For the Scripture says, Everyone who believes on him will not be put to shame, ¹² since there is no distinction between Jew and Greek, because the same Lord of all richly blesses all who call on him. ¹³ For everyone who calls on the name of the Lord will be saved.

TITUS 2:11-14

¹¹ For the grace of God has appeared, bringing salvation for all people, ¹² instructing us to deny godlessness and worldly lusts and to live in a sensible, righteous, and godly way in the present age, ¹³ while we wait for the blessed hope, the appearing of the glory of our great God and Savior, Jesus Christ. ¹⁴ He gave himself for us to redeem us from all lawlessness and to cleanse for himself a people for his own possession, eager to do good works.

WHAT DOES TODAY'S NEW TESTAMENT READING
SAY ABOUT CHRIST AS BOTH PRIEST AND KING?

Use the space below to respond,
reflect on the reading, journal, or record a prayer.

NOW THY GRACIOUS
KINGDOM BRING

DAY 31

DANIEL 2:44-45

⁴⁴ In the days of those kings, the God of the heavens will set up a kingdom that will never be destroyed, and this kingdom will not be left to another people. It will crush all these kingdoms and bring them to an end, but will itself endure forever. ⁴⁵ You saw a stone break off from the mountain without a hand touching it, and it crushed the iron, bronze, fired clay, silver, and gold. The great God has told the king what will happen in the future. The dream is certain, and its interpretation reliable.

ISAIAH 11:1-9

REIGN OF THE DAVIDIC KING

¹ Then a shoot will grow from the stump of Jesse,
and a branch from his roots will bear fruit.
² The Spirit of the LORD will rest on him—
a Spirit of wisdom and understanding,
a Spirit of counsel and strength,
a Spirit of knowledge and of the fear of the LORD.
³ His delight will be in the fear of the LORD.
He will not judge
by what he sees with his eyes,
he will not execute justice
by what he hears with his ears,
⁴ but he will judge the poor righteously
and execute justice for the oppressed of the land.
He will strike the land
with a scepter from his mouth,
and he will kill the wicked
with a command from his lips.
⁵ Righteousness will be a belt around his hips;
faithfulness will be a belt around his waist.

⁶ The wolf will dwell with the lamb,
and the leopard will lie down with the goat.
The calf, the young lion, and the fattened calf will be together,
and a child will lead them.
⁷ The cow and the bear will graze,
their young ones will lie down together,
and the lion will eat straw like cattle.
⁸ An infant will play beside the cobra's pit,
and a toddler will put his hand into a snake's den.
⁹ They will not harm or destroy each other
on my entire holy mountain,

TAKE NOTE

for the land will be as full
of the knowledge of the LORD
as the sea is filled with water.

pause // Underline Daniel 2:44, a description of God's kingdom. //

MARK 4:26-32

THE PARABLE OF THE GROWING SEED

[26] "The kingdom of God is like this," he said. "A man scatters seed on the ground. [27] He sleeps and rises night and day; the seed sprouts and grows, although he doesn't know how. [28] The soil produces a crop by itself—first the blade, then the head, and then the full grain on the head. [29] As soon as the crop is ready, he sends for the sickle, because the harvest has come."

THE PARABLE OF THE MUSTARD SEED

[30] And he said, "With what can we compare the kingdom of God, or what parable can we use to describe it? [31] It's like a mustard seed that, when sown upon the soil, is the smallest of all the seeds on the ground. [32] And when sown, it comes up and grows taller than all the garden plants, and produces large branches, so that the birds of the sky can nest in its shade."

JOHN 18:36-37

[36] "My kingdom is not of this world," said Jesus. "If my kingdom were of this world, my servants would fight, so that I wouldn't be handed over to the Jews. But as it is, my kingdom is not from here."

[37] "You are a king then?" Pilate asked.

"You say that I'm a king," Jesus replied. "I was born for this, and I have come into the world for this: to testify to the truth. Everyone who is of the truth listens to my voice."

EPHESIANS 1:20-21

GOD'S POWER IN CHRIST

[20] He exercised this power in Christ by raising him from the dead and seating him at his right hand in the heavens— [21] far above every ruler and authority, power and dominion, and every title given, not only in this age but also in the one to come.

REVELATION 11:15-17

THE SEVENTH TRUMPET

[15] The seventh angel blew his trumpet, and there were loud voices in heaven saying,

The kingdom of the world has become the kingdom
of our Lord and of his Christ,
and he will reign forever and ever.

[16] The twenty-four elders, who were seated before God on their thrones, fell facedown and worshiped God, [17] saying,

We give you thanks, Lord God, the Almighty,
who is and who was,
because you have taken your great power
and have begun to reign.

HOW DOES TODAY'S READING HELP YOU ANTICIPATE CHRIST'S SECOND ADVENT AND HIS KINGDOM?

Use the space below to respond,
reflect on the reading, journal, or record a prayer.

BY THINE OWN ETERNAL SPIRIT RULE IN ALL OUR HEARTS ALONE

DEUTERONOMY 6:4-5

⁴ Listen, Israel: The LORD our God, the LORD is one. ⁵ Love the LORD your God with all your heart, with all your soul, and with all your strength.

EZEKIEL 36:25-36

²⁵ "I will also sprinkle clean water on you, and you will be clean. I will cleanse you from all your impurities and all your idols. ²⁶ I will give you a new heart and put a new spirit within you; I will remove your heart of stone and give you a heart of flesh. ²⁷ I will place my Spirit within you and cause you to follow my statutes and carefully observe my ordinances. ²⁸ You will live in the land that I gave your ancestors; you will be my people, and I will be your God. ²⁹ I will save you from all your uncleanness. I will summon the grain and make it plentiful, and I will not bring famine on you. ³⁰ I will also make the fruit of the trees and the produce of the field plentiful, so that you will no longer experience reproach among the nations on account of famine.

³¹ "You will remember your evil ways and your deeds that were not good, and you will loathe yourselves for your iniquities and detestable practices. ³² It is not for your sake that I will act—this is the declaration of the Lord GOD—let this be known to you. Be ashamed and humiliated because of your ways, house of Israel!

³³ "This is what the Lord GOD says: On the day I cleanse you from all your iniquities, I will cause the cities to be inhabited, and the ruins will be rebuilt. ³⁴ The desolate land will be cultivated instead of lying desolate in the sight of everyone who passes by. ³⁵ They will say, 'This land that was desolate has become like the garden of Eden. The cities that were once ruined, desolate, and demolished are now fortified and inhabited.' ³⁶ Then the nations that remain around you will know that I, the LORD, have rebuilt what was demolished and have replanted what was desolate. I, the LORD, have spoken and I will do it."

PAUSE HERE

Underline all mentions of the heart in today's Old Testament reading. Draw a box around references to the Spirit.

JOHN 3:1-8

JESUS AND NICODEMUS

¹ There was a man from the Pharisees named Nicodemus, a ruler of the Jews. ² This man came to him at night and said, "Rabbi, we know that you are a teacher who has come from God, for no one could perform these signs you do unless God were with him."

/ TAKE NOTE /

³ Jesus replied, "Truly I tell you, unless someone is born again, he cannot see the kingdom of God."

⁴ "How can anyone be born when he is old?" Nicodemus asked him. "Can he enter his mother's womb a second time and be born?"

⁵ Jesus answered, "Truly I tell you, unless someone is born of water and the Spirit, he cannot enter the kingdom of God. ⁶ Whatever is born of the flesh is flesh, and whatever is born of the Spirit is spirit. ⁷ Do not be amazed that I told you that you must be born again. ⁸ The wind blows where it pleases, and you hear its sound, but you don't know where it comes from or where it is going. So it is with everyone born of the Spirit."

JOHN 16:7-15

⁷ "Nevertheless, I am telling you the truth. It is for your benefit that I go away, because if I don't go away the Counselor will not come to you. If I go, I will send him to you. ⁸ When he comes, he will convict the world about sin, righteousness, and judgment: ⁹ About sin, because they do not believe in me; ¹⁰ about righteousness, because I am going to the Father and you will no longer see me; ¹¹ and about judgment, because the ruler of this world has been judged.

¹² "I still have many things to tell you, but you can't bear them now.

¹³ When the Spirit of truth comes,
he will guide you into all the truth.

For he will not speak on his own, but he will speak whatever he hears. He will also declare to you what is to come. ¹⁴ He will glorify me, because he will take from what is mine and declare it to you. ¹⁵ Everything the Father has is mine. This is why I told you that he takes from what is mine and will declare it to you."

EPHESIANS 1:11-19

¹¹ In him we have also received an inheritance, because we were predestined according to the plan of the one who works out everything in agreement with the purpose of his will, ¹² so that we who had already put our hope in Christ might bring praise to his glory.

¹³ In him you also were sealed with the promised Holy Spirit when you heard the word of truth, the gospel of your salvation, and when you believed. ¹⁴ The Holy Spirit is the down payment of our inheritance, until the redemption of the possession, to the praise of his glory.

PRAYER FOR SPIRITUAL INSIGHT

¹⁵ This is why, since I heard about your faith in the Lord Jesus and your love for all the saints, ¹⁶ I never stop giving thanks for you as I remember you in my prayers. ¹⁷ I pray that the God of our Lord Jesus Christ, the glorious Father, would give you the Spirit of wisdom and revelation in the knowledge of him. ¹⁸ I pray that the eyes of your heart may be enlightened so that you may know what is the hope of his calling, what is the wealth of his glorious inheritance in the saints, ¹⁹ and what is the immeasurable greatness of his power toward us who believe, according to the mighty working of his strength.

2 CORINTHIANS 3:3

You show that you are Christ's letter, delivered by us, not written with ink but with the Spirit of the living God—not on tablets of stone but on tablets of human hearts.

HOW DOES TODAY'S NEW TESTAMENT READING POINT TO THE HOLY SPIRIT'S WORK IN RENEWING OUR HEARTS?

Use the space below to respond,
reflect on the reading, journal, or record a prayer.

_____

_____

_____

_____

_____

_____

_____

_____

_____

_____

_____

_____

_____

_____

_____

_____

_____

_____

"

THE LORD IS COMING,
ALWAYS COMING.
WHEN YOU HAVE EARS TO
HEAR AND EYES TO SEE,
YOU WILL RECOGNIZE HIM
AT ANY MOMENT OF YOUR
LIFE. LIFE IS ADVENT;
LIFE IS RECOGNIZING THE
COMING OF THE LORD.

henri

NOUWEN

COME, THOU LONG-EXPECTED JESUS,

BORN TO SET THY PEOPLE FREE;

FROM OUR FEARS AND SINS RELEASE US;

LET US FIND OUR REST IN THEE.

ISRAEL'S STRENGTH AND CONSOLATION,

HOPE OF ALL THE EARTH THOU ART;

DEAR DESIRE OF EV'RY NATION,

JOY OF EV'RY LONGING HEART.

BORN THY PEOPLE TO DELIVER,

BORN A CHILD, AND YET A KING,

BORN TO REIGN IN US FOREVER,

NOW THY GRACIOUS KINGDOM BRING.

BY THINE OWN ETERNAL SPIRIT RULE
IN ALL OUR HEARTS ALONE;

BY THINE ALL-SUFFICIENT MERIT, RAISE US TO THY GLORIOUS THRONE.

PSALM 14

A PORTRAIT OF SINNERS

For the choir director. Of David.

1 The fool says in his heart, "There's no God."
They are corrupt; they do vile deeds.
There is no one who does good.
2 The LORD looks down from heaven on the human race
to see if there is one who is wise,
one who seeks God.
3 All have turned away;
all alike have become corrupt.
There is no one who does good,
not even one.

4 Will evildoers never understand?
They consume my people as they consume bread;
they do not call on the LORD.

5 Then they will be filled with dread,
for God is with those who are righteous.
6 You sinners frustrate the plans of the oppressed,
but the LORD is his refuge.

7 Oh, that Israel's deliverance would come from Zion!
When the LORD restores the fortunes of his people,
let Jacob rejoice, let Israel be glad.

PAUSE Underline Psalm 14:3, our
condition apart from Christ.

JOHN 19:16-25, 28-30

16 Then he handed him over to be crucified.

THE CRUCIFIXION

Then they took Jesus away. 17 Carrying the cross by himself, he went out to what is called Place of the Skull, which in Aramaic is called *Golgotha*. 18 There they crucified him and two others with him, one on either side, with Jesus in the middle. 19 Pilate also had a sign made and put on the cross. It said: JESUS OF NAZARETH, THE KING OF THE JEWS. 20 Many of the Jews read this sign, because the place where Jesus was crucified was near the city, and it was written in Aramaic, Latin, and Greek. 21 So the chief priests of the Jews said to Pilate, "Don't write, 'The king of the Jews,' but that he said, 'I am the king of the Jews.'"

22 Pilate replied, "What I have written, I have written."

23 When the soldiers crucified Jesus, they took his clothes and divided them into four parts, a part for each soldier. They also took the tunic, which was seamless, woven in one piece from the top. 24 So they said to one another, "Let's not tear it, but cast lots for it, to see who gets it." This happened that the Scripture might be fulfilled that says: They divided my clothes among themselves, and they cast lots for my clothing. This is what the soldiers did.

25 Standing by the cross of Jesus were his mother, his mother's sister, Mary the wife of Clopas, and Mary Magdalene.

…

THE FINISHED WORK OF JESUS

28 After this, when Jesus knew that everything was now finished that the Scripture might be fulfilled, he said, "I'm thirsty." 29 A jar full of sour wine was sitting there; so they fixed a sponge full of sour wine on a hyssop branch and held it up to his mouth.

30 When Jesus had received the sour wine, he said, "It is finished." Then bowing his head, he gave up his spirit.

HEBREWS 10:5-18

5 Therefore, as he was coming into the world, he said:

You did not desire sacrifice and offering,
but you prepared a body for me.
6 You did not delight
in whole burnt offerings and sin offerings.
7 Then I said, "See—

it is written about me
in the scroll—
I have come to do your will, God."

[8] After he says above, You did not desire or delight in sacrifices and offerings, whole burnt offerings and sin offerings (which are offered according to the law), [9] he then says, See, I have come to do your will. He takes away the first to establish the second.

[10] By this will, we have been sanctified through the offering of the body of Jesus Christ once for all time.

[11] Every priest stands day after day ministering and offering the same sacrifices time after time, which can never take away sins. [12] But this man, after offering one sacrifice for sins forever, sat down at the right hand of God. [13] He is now waiting until his enemies are made his footstool. [14] For by one offering he has perfected forever those who are sanctified. [15] The Holy Spirit also testifies to us about this. For after he says:

[16] This is the covenant I will make with them
after those days,

the Lord says,

I will put my laws on their hearts
and write them on their minds,

[17] and I will never again remember

their sins and their lawless acts.

[18] Now where there is forgiveness of these, there is no longer an offering for sin.

EPHESIANS 2:4–9

[4] But God, who is rich in mercy, because of his great love that he had for us, [5] made us alive with Christ even though we were dead in trespasses. You are saved by grace! [6] He also raised us up with him and seated us with him in the heavens in Christ Jesus, [7] so that in the coming ages he might display the immeasurable riches of his grace through his kindness to us in Christ Jesus. [8] For you are saved by grace through faith, and this is not from yourselves; it is God's gift— [9] not from works, so that no one can boast.

PHILIPPIANS 2:5–11

CHRIST'S HUMILITY AND EXALTATION

[5] Adopt the same attitude as that of Christ Jesus,

[6] who, existing in the form of God,
did not consider equality with God
as something to be exploited.
[7] Instead he emptied himself
by assuming the form of a servant,
taking on the likeness of humanity.
And when he had come as a man,
[8] he humbled himself by becoming obedient
to the point of death—
even to death on a cross.
[9] For this reason God highly exalted him
and gave him the name
that is above every name,
[10] so that at the name of Jesus
every knee will bow—
in heaven and on earth
and under the earth—
[11] and every tongue will confess
that Jesus Christ is Lord,
to the glory of God the Father.

WHAT CONFIDENCE DOES TODAY'S NEW TESTAMENT READING GIVE YOU AS YOU WAIT FOR THE SECOND ADVENT?

Use the space below to respond,
reflect on the reading, journal, or record a prayer.

BY THINE ALL-SUFFICIENT MERIT, RAISE US TO THY GLORIOUS THRONE

DAY 34

DANIEL 7:13-14, 27

¹³ I continued watching in the night visions,

and suddenly one like a son of man
was coming with the clouds of heaven.
He approached the Ancient of Days
and was escorted before him.
¹⁴ He was given dominion
and glory and a kingdom,
so that those of every people,
nation, and language
should serve him.
His dominion is an everlasting dominion
that will not pass away,
and his kingdom is one
that will not be destroyed.

…

²⁷ The kingdom, dominion, and greatness of the kingdoms under all of heaven will be given to the people, the holy ones of the Most High. His kingdom will be an everlasting kingdom, and all rulers will serve and obey him.

pause // Underline Daniel 7:27, Daniel's prophecy about the future of those who follow God. //

LUKE 21:25-31, 34-36

THE COMING OF THE SON OF MAN

²⁵ "Then there will be signs in the sun, moon, and stars; and there will be anguish on the earth among nations bewildered by the roaring of the sea and the waves. ²⁶ People will faint from fear and expectation of the things that are coming on the world, because the powers of the heavens will be shaken. ²⁷ Then they will see the Son of Man coming in a cloud with power and great glory. ²⁸ But when these things begin to take place, stand up and lift your heads, because your redemption is near."

THE PARABLE OF THE FIG TREE

²⁹ Then he told them a parable: "Look at the fig tree, and all the trees. ³⁰ As soon as they put out leaves you can see for yourselves and recognize that summer is already near. ³¹ In the same way, when you see these things happening, recognize that the kingdom of God is near."

…

/ TAKE NOTE /

[34] "Be on your guard, so that your minds are not dulled from carousing, drunkenness, and worries of life, or that day will come on you unexpectedly [35] like a trap. For it will come on all who live on the face of the whole earth. [36] But be alert at all times, praying that you may have strength to escape all these things that are going to take place and to stand before the Son of Man."

1 CORINTHIANS 15:50–57

VICTORIOUS RESURRECTION

[50] What I am saying, brothers and sisters, is this: Flesh and blood cannot inherit the kingdom of God, nor can corruption inherit incorruption. [51] Listen, I am telling you a mystery: We will not all fall asleep, but we will all be changed, [52] in a moment, in the twinkling of an eye, at the last trumpet. For the trumpet will sound, and the dead will be raised incorruptible, and we will be changed. [53] For this corruptible body must be clothed with incorruptibility, and this mortal body must be clothed with immortality. [54] When this corruptible body is clothed with incorruptibility, and this mortal body is clothed with immortality, then the saying that is written will take place:

Death has been swallowed up in victory.
[55] Where, death, is your victory?
Where, death, is your sting?

[56] The sting of death is sin, and the power of sin is the law.

[57] But thanks be to God, who gives us the victory through our Lord Jesus Christ!

2 TIMOTHY 2:8–13

[8] Remember Jesus Christ, risen from the dead and descended from David, according to my gospel, [9] for which I suffer to the point of being bound like a criminal. But the word of God is not bound. [10] This is why I endure all things for the elect: so that they also may obtain salvation, which is in Christ Jesus, with eternal glory. [11] This saying is trustworthy:

For if we died with him,
we will also live with him;
[12] if we endure, we will also reign with him;
if we deny him, he will also deny us;
[13] if we are faithless, he remains faithful,
for he cannot deny himself.

REVELATION 5:8–13

THE LAMB IS WORTHY

[8] When he took the scroll, the four living creatures and the twenty-four elders fell down before the Lamb. Each one had a harp and golden bowls filled with incense, which are the prayers of the saints. [9] And they sang a new song:

You are worthy to take the scroll
and to open its seals,
because you were slaughtered,
and you purchased people
for God by your blood
from every tribe and language
and people and nation.
[10] You made them a kingdom
and priests to our God,
and they will reign on the earth.

[11] Then I looked and heard the voice of many angels around the throne, and also of the living creatures and of the elders. Their number was countless thousands, plus thousands of thousands. [12] They said with a loud voice,

Worthy is the Lamb who was slaughtered
to receive power and riches
and wisdom and strength
and honor and glory and blessing!

[13] I heard every creature in heaven, on earth, under the earth, on the sea, and everything in them say,

Blessing and honor and glory and power
be to the one seated on the throne,
and to the Lamb, forever and ever!

HOW IS THE FUTURE FOR BELIEVERS DESCRIBED IN TODAY'S FINAL NEW TESTAMENT READING? HOW CAN THIS ANTICIPATION SHAPE YOUR APPROACH TO THE NEW YEAR?

––––––––––

Use the space below to respond,
reflect on the reading, journal, or record a prayer.

Day 35

GRACE DAY

On this final day of the year,
reflect on your last five weeks
of reading, remembering Jesus's
first coming and anticipating His
promised return. Take time today
to catch up on your reading,
make space for prayer, and rest
in the presence of the Lord.

SO THAT AT
THE name OF JESUS
EVERY knee WILL BOW—
IN heaven AND ON earth
and UNDER THE EARTH—
AND every TONGUE
WILL CONFESS THAT
JESUS CHRIST is LORD,
TO THE glory OF
GOD THE FATHER.

Philippians 2:10–11

THE SECOND SUNDAY

of Christmastide

For we know that the one who raised
the Lord Jesus will also raise us
with Jesus and present us with you.

2 Corinthians 4:14

―――――――

As we conclude this Advent study, read the
words of this hymn as a reflection on all we've
read together. Spend some time in prayer,
giving thanks to Jesus for His first coming and
expressing your longing for His second.

COME, THOU LONG-EXPECTED JESUS,

BORN TO SET THY PEOPLE FREE;

FROM OUR FEARS AND SINS RELEASE US;

LET US FIND OUR REST IN THEE.

ISRAEL'S STRENGTH AND CONSOLATION,

HOPE OF ALL THE EARTH THOU ART;

DEAR DESIRE OF EV'RY NATION,

JOY OF EV'RY LONGING HEART.

BORN THY PEOPLE TO DELIVER,

BORN A CHILD, AND YET A KING,

BORN TO REIGN IN US FOREVER,

NOW THY GRACIOUS KINGDOM BRING.

BY THINE OWN ETERNAL SPIRIT RULE

IN ALL OUR HEARTS ALONE;

BY THINE ALL-SUFFICIENT MERIT,

RAISE US TO THY GLORIOUS THRONE.

words / CHARLES WESLEY / *music* ROWLAND H. PRICHARD /

BENEDICTION

BOTH THE SPIRIT AND THE
BRIDE SAY, "COME!" LET ANYONE
WHO HEARS, SAY, "COME!"
LET THE ONE WHO IS THIRSTY
COME. LET THE ONE WHO
DESIRES TAKE THE WATER OF
LIFE FREELY.
...
HE WHO TESTIFIES ABOUT
THESE THINGS SAYS,
"YES, I AM COMING SOON."

AMEN! COME, LORD JESUS!

Revelation 22:17, 20

FOR THE
record

How did I celebrate Jesus's birth this Advent season?

_____

_____

_____

_____

_____

_____

How did I anticipate Christ's second advent?

_____

_____

_____

_____

_____

_____

_____

WHAT WAS MY FAVORITE CHRISTMAS CAROL TO SING THIS YEAR?

MY FAVORITE DAY IN THIS ADVENT STUDY:

1	2	3	4	5	6
7	8	9	10	11	12
13	14	15	16	17	18
19	20	21	22	23	24
25	26	27	28	29	30
31	32	33	34	35	36

MY FAVORITE SCRIPTURE FROM THIS ADVENT STUDY:

HOW DID THIS STUDY HELP ME CULTIVATE A SENSE OF LONGING FOR CHRIST?

WHAT DID I LEARN THIS ADVENT THAT I WANT TO SHARE WITH SOMEONE ELSE?

HOW WAS CHRISTMAS DAY DIFFERENT THIS YEAR BECAUSE OF THE TIME I SPENT READING GOD'S WORD DURING ADVENT?

What does it look like to live in continued reflection of Jesus being the joy of every longing heart?

_____

_____

_____

_____

_____

_____

_____

_____

_____

_____

_____

in 2022...

How did I see God at work
over the past year?

_____

_____

_____

_____

AN UNEXPECTED JOY:

AN UNEXPECTED SORROW:

MY FAVORITE SHE READS TRUTH STUDY OF 2022:

SOMETHING GOD TAUGHT ME ABOUT
HIS CHARACTER:

I'M MOST PROUD OF:

SOMETHING GOD TAUGHT ME ABOUT MYSELF:

THE HIGHLIGHT OF MY YEAR:

MY PRAYER FOR

2023

_____

_____

_____

_____

_____

_____

_____

_____

_____

_____

_____

_____

_____

_____

DON'T STOP READING NOW—START YOUR YEAR IN SCRIPTURE!

Join us for **The Life of Jesus**, beginning Monday, January 2.

Tips for Memorizing Scripture

At She Reads Truth, we believe Scripture memorization is an important discipline in your walk with God. Committing God's Truth to memory means He can minister to us—and we can minister to others—through His Word no matter where we are. As you approach the Weekly Truth passage in this book, try these memorization tips to see which techniques work best for you!

STUDY IT

Study the passage in its biblical context and ask yourself a few questions before you begin to memorize it: What does this passage say? What does it mean? How would I say this in my own words? What does it teach me about God? Understanding what the passage means helps you know why it is important to carry it with you wherever you go.

Break the passage into smaller sections, memorizing a phrase at a time.

PRAY IT

Use the passage you are memorizing as a prompt for prayer.

WRITE IT

Dedicate a notebook to Scripture memorization and write the passage over and over again.

Diagram the passage after you write it out. Place a square around the verbs, underline the nouns, and circle any adjectives or adverbs. Say the passage aloud several times, emphasizing the verbs as you repeat it. Then do the same thing again with the nouns, then the adjectives and adverbs.

Write out the first letter of each word in the passage somewhere you can reference it throughout the week as you work on your memorization.

Use a whiteboard to write out the passage. Erase a few words at a time as you continue to repeat it aloud. Keep erasing parts of the passage until you have it all committed to memory.

CREATE

If you can, make up a tune for the passage to sing as you go about your day, or try singing it to the tune of a favorite song.

Sketch the passage, visualizing what each phrase would look like in the form of a picture. Or, try using calligraphy or altering the style of your handwriting as you write it out.

Use hand signals or signs to come up with associations for each word or phrase and repeat the movements as you practice.

SAY IT

Repeat the passage out loud to yourself as you are going through the rhythm of your day—getting ready, pouring your coffee, waiting in traffic, or making dinner.

Listen to the passage read aloud to you.

Record a voice memo on your phone and listen to it throughout the day or play it on an audio Bible.

SHARE IT

Memorize the passage with a friend, family member, or mentor. Spontaneously challenge each other to recite the passage, or pick a time to review your passage and practice saying it from memory together.

Send the passage as an encouraging text to a friend, testing yourself as you type to see how much you have memorized so far.

KEEP AT IT!

Set reminders on your phone to prompt you to practice your passage.

Purchase a She Reads Truth Card Set or keep a stack of note cards with Scripture you are memorizing by your bed. Practice reciting what you've memorized previously before you go to sleep, ending with the passages you are currently learning. If you wake up in the middle of the night, review them again instead of grabbing your phone. Read them out loud before you get out of bed in the morning.

Download the free Weekly Truth lock screens for your phone on the She Reads Truth app and read the passage throughout the day when you check your phone.

CSB BOOK ABBREVIATIONS

OLD TESTAMENT

GN Genesis	**JB** Job	**HAB** Habakkuk	**PHP** Philippians
EX Exodus	**PS** Psalms	**ZPH** Zephaniah	**COL** Colossians
LV Leviticus	**PR** Proverbs	**HG** Haggai	**1TH** 1 Thessalonians
NM Numbers	**EC** Ecclesiastes	**ZCH** Zechariah	**2TH** 2 Thessalonians
DT Deuteronomy	**SG** Song of Solomon	**MAL** Malachi	**1TM** 1 Timothy
JOS Joshua	**IS** Isaiah		**2TM** 2 Timothy
JDG Judges	**JR** Jeremiah	**NEW TESTAMENT**	**TI** Titus
RU Ruth	**LM** Lamentations	**MT** Matthew	**PHM** Philemon
1SM 1 Samuel	**EZK** Ezekiel	**MK** Mark	**HEB** Hebrews
2SM 2 Samuel	**DN** Daniel	**LK** Luke	**JMS** James
1KG 1 Kings	**HS** Hosea	**JN** John	**1PT** 1 Peter
2KG 2 Kings	**JL** Joel	**AC** Acts	**2PT** 2 Peter
1CH 1 Chronicles	**AM** Amos	**RM** Romans	**1JN** 1 John
2CH 2 Chronicles	**OB** Obadiah	**1CO** 1 Corinthians	**2JN** 2 John
EZR Ezra	**JNH** Jonah	**2CO** 2 Corinthians	**3JN** 3 John
NEH Nehemiah	**MC** Micah	**GL** Galatians	**JD** Jude
EST Esther	**NAH** Nahum	**EPH** Ephesians	**RV** Revelation

BIBLIOGRAPHY

Arndt, William, Frederick W. Danker, Walter Bauer, and F. Wilbur Gingrich. *A Greek-English Lexicon of the New Testament and Other Early Christian Literature*. Chicago: University of Chicago Press, 2000.

Bauer, Judy. *Advent and Christmas Wisdom from Henri J. M. Nouwen: Daily Scripture and Prayers Together with Nouwen's Own Words*. Liguori: Liguori Publications, 2004.

Bonhoeffer, Dietrich. *God Is in the Manger: Reflections on Advent and Christmas*. Louisville: Westminster John Knox Press, 2010.

The Book of Common Prayer and Administration of the Sacraments and other Rites and Ceremonies of the Church. New York: Church Publishing, Inc., 1789.

Brink, Emily Ruth, and Bertus Frederick Polman. *Psalter Hymnal Handbook*. Grand Rapids: CRC Publications, 1998.

Browning, Daniel C., Jr. "Minerals and Metals." In *Holman Illustrated Bible Dictionary*, edited by Chad Brand, Charles Draper, Archie England, Steve Bond, E. Ray Clendenen, and Trent C. Butler. Nashville: Holman Bible Publishers, 2003.

Elwell, Walter A., and Barry J. Beitzel. "Census." In *Baker Encyclopedia of the Bible*, 1:420–21. Grand Rapids: Baker Book House, 1988.

Elwell, Walter A., and Barry J. Beitzel. "Manger." In *Baker Encyclopedia of the Bible*, 2:1391–92. Grand Rapids: Baker Book House, 1988.

France, R. T. *Matthew: An Introduction and Commentary*. Tyndale New Testament Commentaries. Downers Grove: InterVarsity Press, 1985.

Grant, George, and Gregory Wilbur. *Christmas Spirit: The Joyous Stories, Carols, Feasts, and Traditions of the Season*. Nashville: Cumberland House Publishing,

Jackman, Ian. *A Christmas Miscellany: A Victorian Holiday Treasury*. New York: Random House Reference, 2005.

Knight, George W. "Bethlehem." In *Holman Illustrated Bible Dictionary*, edited by Chad Brand, Charles Draper, Archie England, Steve Bond, E. Ray Clendenen, and Trent C. Butler. Nashville: Holman Bible Publishers, 2003.

Knox, James W. "Frankincense." In *The Lexham Bible Dictionary*, edited by John D. Barry, David Bomar, Derek R. Brown, Rachel Klippenstein, Douglas Mangum, Carrie Sinclair Wolcott, Lazarus Wentz, Elliot Ritzema, and Wendy Widder. Bellingham: Lexham Press, 2016.

Knox, James W. "Myrrh." In *The Lexham Bible Dictionary*, edited by John D. Barry, David Bomar, Derek R. Brown, Rachel Klippenstein, Douglas Mangum, Carrie Sinclair Wolcott, Lazarus Wentz, Elliot Ritzema, and Wendy Widder. Bellingham: Lexham Press, 2016.

McMains, Matthew J. "Hosts." In *The Lexham Bible Dictionary*, edited by John D. Barry, David Bomar, Derek R. Brown, Rachel Klippenstein, Douglas Mangum, Carrie Sinclair Wolcott, Lazarus Wentz, Elliot Ritzema, and Wendy Widder. Bellingham: Lexham Press, 2016.

Morris, Leon. *Luke: An Introduction and Commentary*. Vol. 3. Tyndale New Testament Commentaries. Downers Grove: InterVarsity Press, 1988.

Parrott, Charles Joshua. "Manger." In *The Lexham Bible Dictionary*, edited by John D. Barry, David Bomar, Derek R. Brown, Rachel Klippenstein, Douglas Mangum, Carrie Sinclair Wolcott, Lazarus Wentz, Elliot Ritzema, and Wendy Widder. Bellingham: Lexham Press, 2016.

Strauss, Mark L. "Messiah." In *The Lexham Bible Dictionary*, edited by John D. Barry, David Bomar, Derek R. Brown, Rachel Klippenstein, Douglas Mangum, Carrie Sinclair Wolcott, Lazarus Wentz, Elliot Ritzema, and Wendy Widder. Bellingham: Lexham Press, 2016.

Wulf, Frank D. "Decree," in *Eerdmans Dictionary of the Bible*, edited by David Noel Freedman, Allen C. Myers, and Astrid B. Beck. Grand Rapids: W.B. Eerdmans, 2000.

Stay in God's Word.

The She Reads Truth Subscription Box is an easy way to have a consistent Bible reading plan.

Every month, we'll send you a brand new Study Book filled with daily Scripture readings and all sorts of beautiful extra features to help you read the Bible. All you have to do is open your book, read with us today, and read with us again tomorrow—it's that simple!